Critical Literacy and Writer's Workshop

Bringing Purpose and Passion to Student Writing

LEE HEFFERNAN
Bloomington, Indiana, USA

INTERNATIONAL
Reading Association
800 BARKSDALE ROAD, PO BOX 8139
NEWARK, DE 19714-8139, USA
www.reading.org

The International Reading Association attempts, through its publications, to provide a forum for a wide spectrum of opinions on reading. This policy permits divergent viewpoints without implying the endorsement of the Association.

Director of Publications   Joan M. Irwin
Editorial Director, Books and Special Projects   Matthew W. Baker
Managing Editor   Shannon Benner
Permissions Editor   Janet S. Parrack
Acquisitions and Communications Coordinator   Corinne M. Mooney
Associate Editor, Books and Special Projects   Sara J. Murphy
Assistant Editor   Charlene M. Nichols
Administrative Assistant   Michele Jester
Senior Editorial Assistant   Tyanna L. Collins
Production Department Manager   Iona Muscella
Supervisor, Electronic Publishing   Anette Schütz
Senior Electronic Publishing Specialist   Cheryl J. Strum
Electronic Publishing Specialist   R. Lynn Harrison
Proofreader   Elizabeth C. Hunt

Project Editor   Janet S. Parrack

Cover Design   Linda Steere; photograph by Creatas

Web addresses in this book were correct as of the publication date but may have become inactive or otherwise modified since that time. If you notice a deactivated or changed Web address, please e-mail books@reading.org with the words "Website Update" in the subject line. In your message, specify the Web link, the book title, and the page number on which the link appears.

Library of Congress Cataloging-in-Publication Data
Heffernan, Lee, 1960-
  Critical literacy and writer's workshop : bringing purpose and passion to student writing / Lee Heffernan.
      p. cm.
  Includes bibliographical references and index.
  ISBN 0-87207-541-9 (alk. paper)
  1. English language—Composition and exercises—Study and teaching (Elementary)—United States. 2. Language arts (Elementary)—Social aspects—United States. 3. Literacy—Social aspects—United States. I. Title.
  LB1576.H3315 2004
  372.62'3—dc22
                                                                                          2004002142

For Peter, my collaborator in all things

Contents

Preface

I once taught a third-grade student named Mark who happened to be crazy about the movie *Jurassic Park*. Every day during writer's workshop, he would write his own slightly altered version of the movie. After he wrote several of these, I told Mark to move on to a new topic, but the kid was tenacious. Somehow, despite my best efforts during writing conferences, dinosaur theme parks kept sneaking into his pieces. In the fall of the following year, as I walked through our school library, I spied Mark's name at the top of a piece of paper slowly slipping out of the printer. Curious, I stopped to see what he was working on. As I watched Mark's title emerge—"The Lost World of Jurassic Park, The Next Adventure"—I felt a rush of frustration that only teachers can know. But I had to laugh as I wondered how many versions of *Jurassic Park* Mark would write before his fourth-grade teacher tired of his obsession.

If you teach writing to students in the elementary grades, you may have your own tales of topic recycling. You probably have read your share of stories based on the latest hit movies or video games. Or if you have encouraged student writers to focus on personal, real-life writing, you may be familiar with some of the same personal narratives I've read over the years, such as "My Dog Sammy," "Best Gift Ever," "Baseball Card Mania," "The Big Gymnastics Meet," and the all-time classic, "Visiting My Cousin."

Over the past 20 years of elementary school teaching, I have read enough stories about new bikes, baby sisters, and triumphant baseball games to last a lifetime. "At least they're writing," my coworkers and I have sighed when we have shared our frustrations about the repetitive, recycled topics of student writing that we encounter.

This book describes a change in the type of writing that third-grade students produced as critical literacy practices were introduced in writer's workshop. Critical literacy has been defined in different ways by different researchers. For example, Seely-Flint, Lewison, and Van Sluys (2002) review

> a range of definitions from 30 years of research and professional literature and have synthesized these definitions into the following four dimensions
>
> • Disrupting the commonplace
> • Interrogating multiple viewpoints

- Focusing on sociopolitical issues
- Taking action and promoting social justice. (p. 382)

Instead of simply recording life events, critically literate readers and writers use text to get something done in the world.

Incorporating the dimensions of critical literacy into writer's workshop leads to an expanded conceptualization of student writing. Writing becomes not only a recording of personal interests and inquiries but also a form of social action—a connection between the personal and the social. When compared to the dimensions listed above, titles like "My Dog Sammy" and "Jurassic Park Adventure" indicate a lack of relevance as well as a passive stance on the part of student writers.

Organization of This Book

Chapter 1 begins the story of a yearlong project in my third-grade class that involved my attempts to integrate critical literacy and writer's workshop by reading books to my students that focused on social issues. The chapter includes an expanded bibliography of the texts that I used to start my students thinking, talking, and writing about social issues.

Chapter 2 outlines some critiques of writer's workshop that have been explored by leading literacy researchers. The chapter also includes the surprising results of a survey I administered to third and sixth graders in order to learn more about their perspectives on writing and writer's workshop.

Chapter 3 describes the first weeks of writer's workshop as students began to choose their initial topics. Because the social-issue texts had generated emotional and serious conversation, I used them as a springboard for student writing in writer's workshop. The chapter also discusses some of the problems associated with writing personal narratives.

Chapter 4 presents six classroom sessions for analyzing a social-issue text, describing procedures for giving students ways to respond to text through writing and conversation.

Chapter 5 emphasizes the importance of student talk about social-issue texts. As students discussed these texts, they wrote about connections between the texts and their own lives. Classroom conversation, social-issue texts, and notebook entries became valuable resources that students drew upon to write their own stories.

Chapter 6 offers a snapshot of the classroom as students began sifting through their notebooks for themes and important vignettes to include in their stories. A focus on themes rather than topics allowed students to move beyond the retelling of personal stories as they wove their personal lives and their social concerns into their writing.

Chapter 7 describes some of the changes I made to the structure of writer's workshop, for example, using books by influential writers as a source of minilesson material, enhancing the revision process to focus on thematic clarity, and instituting a new way for students to share their stories during writer's workshop. The chapter shows an example of the students' revision process.

Chapter 8 demonstrates how the students' stories written during writer's workshop provided opportunities for discussing questions about cultural and social issues. Two fiction stories written by students are presented. In excerpts from these stories, social issues are blended with the stuff of kid culture in an attempt to direct reader attention toward real-world issues faced by young children in and out of school.

Chapter 9 describes the creation of a new genre of writing called "social narrative" (Heffernan & Lewison, 2003). Rather than looking inward at individual experiences, students drew on a range of resources to write fiction stories, combining events from their own lives with shared themes generated through classroom activities. The students revisited the use of fiction as a means of analyzing and rewriting the social world of school. Student writers came to view writing as a form of social action and joined together as a writing collective to broadcast their concerns through the writing of social narratives.

Chapter 10 explores two often-asked questions about critical literacy and the writer's workshop. I also discuss the importance for all students to be given opportunities to discuss and inquire about their social issues and concerns.

All the chapters outline the potential benefits of bringing a critical or sociological perspective to writer's workshop. Harste and Leland (2000) write that "teachers who re-imagine teaching as a set of critical practices disrupt the normative patterns of society and open up spaces for new voices to be heard" (p. 6). *Critical Literacy and Writer's Workshop* describes how putting critical practices in place shook up the norms of writer's workshop and allowed new stories to be written and told. This book is written for all readers with an interest in critical literacy, but especially for those writing teachers who have stayed up late on countless nights, reading about broken arms, pet cats, and rock collections.

Acknowledgments

Friends and family gave me incredible support as I worked as both a teacher and a graduate student in recent years. My parents, Ann and Dan Heffernan, and my six siblings encouraged me every step of the way. Good friend and coworker Judy Williams provided resources and insightful advice during all stages of writing. Over the years, the wonderful third graders in room 204 and their parents expressed interest and gave me much-appreciated feedback. My two quite extraordinary children, Rosalyn and Quinn, cheered me every day and kept this work exciting and fun. I appreciate feedback and assistance from International Reading Association reviewers and editors, especially Matt Baker and Janet Parrack.

My work has been shaped by conversations with all my Indiana University colleagues and professors. Many thanks to Dr. Chalmer Thompson for conversing with me through our race dialog project. And thanks to Dr. Jerry Harste for his many invitations to imagine what literacy can be. I especially acknowledge the generous support, guidance, and friendship of Dr. Mitzi Lewison throughout the entire process that went into researching and writing this book.

—LH

CHAPTER I

Taking the First Steps Toward Critical Literacy

I n the mid-1980s, I became a writing-process groupie. The authoring cycle
of Harste, Short, and Burke (1988) turned my textbook-driven English
class into an exciting and busy writer's workshop, where kids selected their
own writing topics, drafted, revised, conferred, and published. I read
everything I could get my hands on by Donald Graves (1983), Nancy Atwell
(1987), and Lucy Calkins (1986). I traveled to hear them speak at conferences.
I attended readings by published authors, joined a local writers' group, and
carried a writer's notebook everywhere I went.

Over a decade later, writer's workshop was still in place as a curricular
framework, but despite my passion for writing, I often felt less than successful
as a writing teacher. Not only were students churning out the same kinds of
stories, but the amount of time and effort I put into planning minilessons,
conferring with individual students, and assessing student writing did not seem
to lead to much improvement in the quality of student drafts. My students, for
the most part, were avid readers, but I often had the nagging feeling that they
were capable of more when it came to writing. This feeling grew as I learned
more about critical literacy.

Opening the Classroom Door to Critical Literacy

In 1999, I enrolled in a course titled Literacies and Differences. The course
taught by Jerry Harste involved a project in which I read and discussed with third
graders in my classroom books from a bibliography of social-issue texts to which
I have added (see Table 1). These texts focused on difference, marginalization,
and social action, presenting "complex social problems" without "happily ever
after" endings (Leland, Harste, Oceipka, Lewison, & Vasquez, 1999, p. 70). The
course participants took field notes for shared analysis.

I was uneasy about using the texts from the bibliography because many
dealt with fairly serious social issues, which I feared might frighten or upset

TABLE 1.   Bibliography of Social-Issue Texts and Topics

Title	Topics
From Slave Ship to Freedom Road (Lester, 1998)	Slavery, separation of families, Underground Railroad, hate crimes
"Where Does Hate Come From?" Bloomington, Indiana, Human Rights Commission Essay Contest	Hate crimes, hate speech, our own treatment of other people, ignorance, fear of differences
Whitewash (Shange, 1997)	Racial violence, power vs. weakness, power of group response
Your Move (Bunting, 1998)	Gangs, guns, working parents
Sarah, Plain and Tall (MacLachlan, 1987)	Women's work, marriage, freedom to choose
Journey to Freedom (Wright, 1994)	Underground Railroad, putting cash value on people, bounty hunters
A Lion to Guard Us (Bulla, 1989)	Child labor, women's clothing, gender, and job issues
Ida Early Comes Over the Mountain (Burch, 1990)	
Skylark (MacLachlan, 1997)	
The Bobbin Girl (McCully, 1996)	Child labor, gender issues, speaking in public
Just Juice (Hesse, 1998)	Poverty, literacy, ways of learning
"High Rents in Bloomington" (*The Herald-Times*, January 1999)	High rents, interaction between the university and the town, renting versus owning homes
Bloomers (Blumberg, 1996)	Dress, public speaking and women's roles
Ian's Walk (Lears, 1998)	Autism, individual expression, civil rights, communicating
Our Brother Has Down's Syndrome (Cairo, Cairo, & Cairo, 1985)	Learning, teasing
"Kosovo's Sorrow" (*Time for Kids*, April 16, 1999)	Consequences of bombing, war, ethnic cleansing, religious differences, being forced to flee, separation of families
Sadako and the Thousand Paper Cranes (Coerr, 1979)	Consequences of bombing, illness, innocent victims, peace
The Music of Dolphins (Hesse, 1996) *Lost Star: The Story of Amelia Earhart* (Lauber, 1990)	Women's work vs. men's work, language, freedom, alcoholism
Yang the Youngest and His Terrible Ear (Namioka, 1994)	
The Day the Earth Was Silent (McGuffee, 1997)	Children and power
One More Border (Kaplan & Tanaka, 1998)	Religious oppression, being forced to flee
Passage to Freedom: The Sugihara Story (Mochizuki, 1997)	Holocaust, being forced to flee, going against the government

Adapted from Leland et al. (1999)

students and raise concerns among parents about the books' contents. As I read through the bibliography, I put check marks next to the books with seemingly less controversial topics to read aloud to my students.

Learning About Critical Literacy

Since taking the course, my understanding of critical literacy has evolved, but the shared inquiry involved in this graduate course laid the foundation for my awareness of how critical literacy practices work to engage readers and writers in actively analyzing and critiquing the connections between personal life and societal structures.

Shannon (1995) describes critical literacy as a literacy that brings with it the freedom to explore and act on our past, present, and future. Comber (2001) writes that critical literacies involve "people using language to exercise power, to enhance everyday life in schools and communities, and to question practices of privilege and injustice" (p. 1). Luke and Freebody (1997) call for redefining reading by using a sociological rather than a psychological model. A psychological model focuses on the individual student's skills, choices, and background knowledge, while a sociological model highlights that "teaching and learning to read is about teaching and learning standpoints, cultural expectations, norms of social actions and consequences" (pp. 208–209). Critical literacy, then, involves reflection and action. Literacy becomes a tool for analyzing our social worlds.

My students knew how to employ a psychological model of writing and individually explored their personal lives and interests through their reading and writing. A more sociological model of writing would include practices in which writers draw on their social and cultural lives to analyze and critique the world around them.

Experimenting With Critical Literacy

Although initially I was uneasy about using the texts outlined in the course bibliography, my expanding understanding of critical literacy enabled me to confront my assumptions about appropriate texts for children.

At one point, the school media specialist gave me the book *From Slave Ship to Freedom Road* (Lester, 1998) because she thought it tied in with the books on the course bibliography. As I looked through the book, I was horrified by the description of the brutality endured by African people during 300 years of slavery. Unable to finish reading the book, I decided not to read it to my class.

As I read more about critical literacy, I picked up the book and tried reading it again, wondering if I could face my fears about using it with students. I had never realized that the slaves had been stacked and chained for months aboard ship, urinating and defecating on themselves and on one another. And the description of slaves being thrown into the ocean when they got sick on the journey made me feel ill. I was too upset by these sad facts to appreciate the richness of this remarkable text—Lester's creative use of imagination exercises for different groups of readers, the mix of first- and third-person narratives, the striking oil painting illustrations, and the elements of hope in this story of courageous resistance.

While I struggled with my emotional reaction to Lester's book in light of my developing understanding of critical literacy, an experience with my daughter forced me to confront my assumptions about this book. A first grader at the time, Rosalyn came home from school and told me, "I have to do an inquiry project. I really want to do it on milk—like when did people figure out it was a good thing to drink." Off we trekked to the library. We found a book titled *Milk: The Fight for Purity* (Giblin, 1986). As Rosalyn listened, I skimmed through the introduction, reading passages to her about milk's history. One section described the export of dairy cows to the American colonies. A ship was built especially to transport the cows as carefully and cleanly as possible, with individual stalls for each cow. The stalls contained boxes of sand for the cows to stand in so that they would not fall or lurch and that made it easier to dispose of the cows' waste. Out of 300 cows that made that journey, only one died. Ironically, this ship sailed during the same years of the slave trade described in Lester's book.

The coincidence of encountering these two books in the same week made me reflect on my complicity in perpetuating the status quo by choosing safe, happy books for my curriculum and rejecting others. What did it mean for me and for my students when I rejected texts about oppression and injustice?

In response to my own question, I decided to begin the course inquiry project by reading *From Slave Ship to Freedom Road* to my third graders. At first, the students took somewhat cavalier stances to the content:

Jesse: If a slave was sick, he might make others sick, so it's better if he's thrown overboard.

Alec (looking at a picture of a slave auction): They look like they're in pretty good shape to me. (Heffernan & Lewison, 2000, p. 16)

Later, however, when the students worked with partners to fill out response sheets about the book, their written responses showed that they had more to say. In fact, I was surprised by the information they shared (see Figure 1a).

FIGURE 1a.   Student's Writing Sample

CRITICAL READING	
Something important we want to remember about this book: How black people where treated. How they would be thrown in the sea.	An anomaly: Something that we did not expect or something that surprised us: The way they were shiped. How they where haged and whiped.
A question we have is: Why did they juge people by the coler of ther skin? Why would they split family.	A connection we have with our world today is: Sometimes people in school treat oter people badley.

FIGURE 1b. Student's Writing Sample

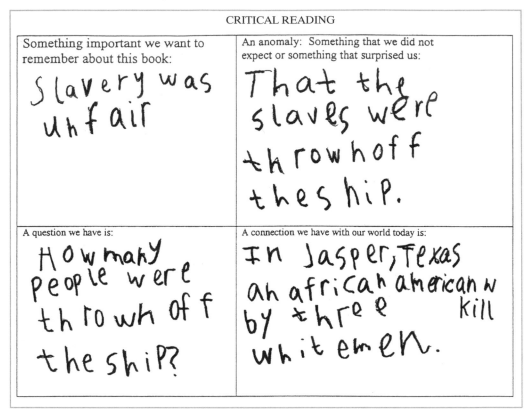

CRITICAL READING

Something important we want to remember about this book:	An anomaly: Something that we did not expect or something that surprised us:
Slavery was unfair	That the slaves were throwhoff the ship.
A question we have is:	A connection we have with our world today is:
How many people were throwh off the ship?	In Jasper, Texas an african american w by three kill white men.

Two boys wrote about the death by dragging of an African American man in Jasper, Texas, USA, which had occurred during the school year (see Figure 1b). Many of the students wrote comments about hate crimes in Bloomington, Indiana, USA, because we had discussed hate crimes previously in connection with an incident in our town earlier in the school year.

Over three to four days, we discussed the book at length. As students met in small groups to discuss the book, their conversations were lengthy and deep. The students were not traumatized—they were engaged and serious as they talked about slavery and racism.

These first steps on my journey toward looking at curriculum through a critical lens made me aware of the potential strength of using social-issue texts in my classroom. It became clear to me that not only could the students talk about tough issues but also that they were ready and willing to do so. My students and I went on to read and discuss approximately 20 more social-issue texts during the course inquiry project. These young students—8 and 9 years old—had opinions about topics that most people would consider too complex or disturbing for children.

Connections in Texts, Connections in the Classroom

Because of the complex nature of class discussions, the students were supported in their thinking about social issues by their discussions with one another and by comparing and presenting information from previous conversations. Rather than simply asking "Why?" when injustice or unfairness were discussed—Why would someone hand out hate literature? Why would someone kill someone because of skin color?—the students pointed to the similarities in the stories of oppression.

As the students' thinking skills developed, the classroom dynamics began to change. A new context developed for dealing with social problems within the classroom. If students treated one another disrespectfully, someone in the group would inevitably interrupt with "Hey, that's hate speech!" The students appeared to be excited and emotionally charged during this time. At classroom morning meetings, students shifted from telling personal stories about lost teeth or weekend plans to sharing news items. Students brought up such issues as the student murders at Columbine High School in Colorado, the bombing of Kosovo that resulted in civilian deaths, and an oil tanker spill in the Persian Gulf. During a conversation about the war in Kosovo, I said to the students, "Some adults think this is too upsetting for us to be talking about in school. What do you think?" Many students shouted out comments such as "We already know!" and "We know about this stuff!" The natural altruism of the students became more and more apparent through the work with the social-issue texts. Our work with these texts provided space for all of us to act as caring, involved citizens. The student conversations about justice themes, although frequently controversial, had made school less artificial and less insular.

Concluding Thoughts

Although I have spent most of my teaching career as a writing-process teacher, I have gradually adopted a more critical, or sociological, view of literacy. In order to take the first steps toward a more critical stance as a teacher, I had to face my fears and question my own assumptions about which books and topics were appropriate for use in my classroom. As I introduced students to books with social-issue themes, the classroom became a place in which serious issues were discussed. Ideas from these books filtered into other parts of the curriculum and brought about an overall change in classroom atmosphere.

Writer's workshop, however, seemed to be unaffected by this reading and talking about social issues. I observed a mismatch between the superficial pieces written during writer's workshop and the sophisticated conversations that were taking place about books such as *From Slave Ship to Freedom Road*. This mismatch led me to ask two questions: (1) How can writer's workshop be part of a critical curriculum? (2) Can a critical lens be used to change the ways children write during writer's workshop? This book is the story of how I worked to find answers to these two questions. I started my journey toward critical literacy with some doubts and trepidation, but these fears dissipated as I came to see power and passion filtering into writer's workshop as students used writing to influence their readers.

CHAPTER 2

Viewing Writer's Workshop
Through a Critical Lens

C ritical literacy practices brought complex, challenging conversations into the curriculum of my third-grade classroom. The students' interest and engagement in these conversations demonstrated to me that third graders had many concerns about their world in and out of school. Surprisingly, however, there was no carryover of these interests to writer's workshop, and kids continued to write about personal interests and events. I tried to think of ways to bring social issues into the writer's workshop as I had with the reading curriculum.

I found that many literacy researchers have critiqued writer's workshop and have pointed out ways in which writer's workshop divides students and prevents writers from analyzing how texts work to silence particular perspectives. According to Lankshear and McLaren (1993), "rewriting the world" is a key element of critical literacy:

> In addressing critical literacy we are concerned with the extent to which, and the ways in which, actual and possible social practices and conceptions of reading and writing enable human subjects to understand and engage the politics of daily life in the quest for a more truly democratic social order. Among other things, critical literacy makes possible a more adequate and accurate "reading" of the world, on the basis of which, as Freire and others put it, people can enter into "rewriting" the world into a formation in which their interests, identities, and legitimate aspirations are more fully present and are present more equally. (p. xviii)

I wanted to know more about how writing could be used to "rewrite the world." I suggested that items discussed in the classroom morning meeting might make excellent writing topics, but the kids did not take me up on these suggestions. Instead, one young writer, Harrison, wrote a piece that forced me to finally acknowledge that changes were needed in the way I taught writing.

The Straw That Broke Pokémon's Back

Although an extremely proficient reader, Harrison was a very reluctant writer. He wasted time during writer's workshop and produced far fewer drafts than other students. One morning before school had begun, Harrison walked into the classroom, sat down at his desk, took out paper and pencil, and started writing up a storm. Stunned and overjoyed, I left him alone, not wanting to jinx this miraculous event. Later, during writer's workshop, I asked Harrison about his piece. "I'm working on a story about Pokémon" (a popular electronic game), he told me. Because of too many experiences, such as the one with Mark described in the Preface, I had imposed restrictions on students' fiction writing, urging students to write personal narratives during writer's workshop. Although I wasn't thrilled with it, I accepted Harrison's topic choice because he had already written several paragraphs and seemed extremely motivated to continue writing. Harrison worked on his Pokémon piece during three workshop sessions, in addition to other times during the school day, spending almost five hours on the piece. It was a rare treat to have this easily distracted student occupied during writer's workshop.

After several days of whirlwind writing, Harrison suddenly lost interest in the piece. He told me he was now thinking of a new topic. When I suggested that he read part of his Pokémon story to classmates to get some revision ideas, he declined. Later, when the class was at recess, I noticed that some pages of Harrison's story, shoved into his desk before leaving for lunch, had fallen to the floor. I walked over to rescue the pages and put them in his writing folder. I shouldn't have been surprised when I started reading, but I was. The first page began

> Hi I am Blain. Go Arkanine. Go Pikachu. Pikachu Thunder shock! Go Rapidash: Thunderbolt. Go Growlith. Pikachu thunder. We win! Harrison rescued Fireblast.
> Let's go to Viridian City. What? Ivysaur is evolving! Ivysaur evolved into Venasaur. There's Pallet Town. Let's go to the house. There's the Viridian Gym. Go Rhydon.

The piece went on in a similar way for five more pages. Although Harrison had enjoyed writing this text, he clearly had no emotional attachment to it. He easily could have written "GAME OVER" across the paper and tossed it in the trashcan.

Harrison was not typical of writers in my class; he represents an extreme case of the potential ways in which students' selection of topics allows them to alienate themselves through the retelling of established mass media narratives. Students who write personal narratives about life events also are writing to retell, rather than to interpret or disrupt the commonplace.

Writing the World: Critiques of Writer's Workshop

On the surface, writer's workshop seems to enable students to make their voices heard through their writing. Students choose their own topics. They interact with peers during writing conferences. But writer's workshop is not always as innocent or as democratic as it would appear. Students frequently write pieces that are full of stereotypes and bias as they replicate television shows or movies they have seen. An additional "underside" (Lensmire, 1994, p. 2) of the workshop is the way in which students use their writing to gain status and to exclude classmates. Lensmire (1994) examines this "underside" of writer's workshop and the "gender divisions and informal hierarchies of status and power" that shape "the production and sharing of texts" (p. 2). Australian researchers Comber and Cormack (1995) also share concerns about writing-process classrooms:

> In some classrooms, children's writing is treated as sacred. Sexist, racist and violent writing is published simply because it is a child's product.... With a focus on the individual, there is not necessarily an awareness of students as gendered, cultured and politically situated people and the negative consequences of literate practices are not considered. (p. 4)

Although with my own students' writing, gender differences had been obvious and constant, my belief in student ownership of writing kept me from confronting this issue head on. Unless a story was extremely violent or contained explicit sexism, I did not speak to students about the ways in which their writing was stereotyped. Later, I read that gender stereotyping is common in writing-process classrooms:

> Young writers do not operate freely outside gender ideology, and their choices are not simply personal and individual. As a consequence, free choice in writing topics tacitly encourages children to reproduce gender stereotypes as they are culturally defined. (Kamler, 1993, p. 95)

Researchers Soo Hoo and Brown (1994) report that students discuss and debate social issues in their group meetings, but during writer's workshop they frequently write stories that are "flat and lifeless" (p. 100):

> To our dismay, social action through student voice did not carry over into student writing. Instead, what they (students) wrote about were things they thought would make good stories. They drew their inspiration from a shared culture, not the one cultivated in the classroom community, but the one they shared as nine- and ten-year olds in Cerritos: the culture of Nintendo, X-men and the Baby-Sitters Club. These were the story topics of choice. (p. 100)

Soo Hoo and Brown also pose several questions for their own inquiry study about how to bring social action into the writer's workshop:

> What should the teacher's role be in guiding students to write about social issues? Whose passivity is being reflected here? Theirs or ours?
>
> How could the teacher help students see the value of their personal experiences and their worlds without taking away the ownership of the writing?
>
> Will a social agenda emerge naturally in writing or does the teacher have to do something?
>
> Is writing about issues more risky because it's more personal?
>
> Is this observed passivity in writing something that happens because of the way schools are organized?
>
> Is the writing workshop an appropriate place for raising social and personal issues? (pp. 101–102)

These questions echoed my own. I felt that writer's workshop *was* an appropriate place for raising social issues, but I wondered how students would react to this kind of writing. Teachers' respect for student ownership of text may create a lack of action on the part of teachers even though they are fully aware of the irrelevance of students' writing.

Surveying Students: Why Write?

Throughout the 1990s, our school had made writing a schoolwide goal with a focus on writing process and publication of student work and with every student maintaining a writing portfolio. To gather information about the students' perceptions of writer's workshop, I designed a survey about the problematic issues explicated by Lensmire (1994). I surveyed 3 third-grade and 2 sixth-grade classes. Fifty-three students in third grade and 56 students in sixth grade took the written survey, which included four questions about writing. This informal survey confirmed many of my thoughts about writer's workshop, but certain results surprised me.

The Survey Says

Because writer's workshop had always been popular in my class, I predicted that most students would say that they enjoyed it.

QUESTION 1: DO YOU LIKE WRITER'S WORKSHOP?

Response	Grade 3		Grade 6	
	Number	Percent	Number	Percent
Yes	45	85%	32	57%
No	5	9%	18	32%
Mixed	3	6%	6	11%

WHY OR WHY NOT?

Yes responses	Grade 3	Yes responses	Grade 6
It's fun/I like to write.	29	It's fun/I like to write.	16
Comments about enjoying choice	9	Lets me express myself.	7
Other	7	Other	9

No responses	Grade 3	No responses	Grade 6
I don't like to write.	3	Prompts don't interest me.	8
I'm not good at writing.	1	I don't like writing.	8
Other	1	Other	2

As shown, 85% of third graders enjoyed writer's workshop, but this percentage decreased fairly dramatically in sixth grade. Of course, if you've taught sixth graders, this isn't surprising. One sixth grader who did not enjoy writer's workshop said, "I've done it my whole school career and I like to do different things." Although this was only one response, when coupled with the fact that 32% of sixth graders did not enjoy writer's workshop, I had to wonder if over time the workshop became tedious for students. The fact that prompt writing becomes more prevalent in the upper grades, undoubtedly as a result of state-mandated writing tests, may also be a factor in turning off students from writing.

Question 2 also was fairly straightforward—aimed at student awareness of the purpose of writer's workshop.

QUESTION 2: WHY DO YOU THINK WE HAVE WRITER'S WORKSHOP AS PART OF OUR SCHOOL DAY?

Response	Grade 3		Response	Grade 6	
	Number	Percent*		Number	Percent
It helps you learn to be a better writer.	38	72%	It helps you learn to be a better writer.	40	71%
It helps you learn mechanics/editing.	6	11%	It's necessary for life.	4	7%
Other	9	17%	Other	12	21%

*Figures rounded to whole numbers

The majority of students in both grade levels felt that the purpose of writer's workshop was to learn to write better. This perception holds some validity in that writers generally do improve their writing skills by writing daily. But there are other reasons for writing that have not been emphasized enough in writing classrooms. As a reading teacher, I probably did a better job of emphasizing a range of purposes for daily reading. I have talked to students about reading using comments such as

> Reading can take you to faraway worlds.
>
> A good book can change your life. Books are important.
>
> You'll be able to do anything if you're a good reader.

I have always pitched reading as a powerful resource for students but have not always presented writing in a similar way because in the past I did not regard school writing as a resource that students could use to analyze the world and influence readers. My predilection for personal narrative pieces evolved because I had not had good results with students writing fiction. However, the personal narrative pieces had become a bit like collections of photographs—snapshots of favorite people and places—interesting for a while but bringing to mind the clichéd image of relatives bringing slides of their vacations for after-dinner viewing.

Harste, Short, and Burke (1988) consider the creation of new meaning to be crucial to the authoring process: "We would argue that the element of the authoring process that is most important for learning is not meaning maintenance, but meaning generation" (p. 10). The students were using the authoring process to maintain or record meaning rather than as a tool for "discovering new connections between existing ideas" (p. 10).

Although most students preferred fiction writing, I felt I had to move away from personal narrative writing because these pieces, as they were being written in my classroom, limited students' views of the potential that writing could have as a tool for influencing readers.

QUESTION 3: WHAT'S YOUR FAVORITE KIND OF WRITING TO DO?

Response	Grade 3		Response	Grade 6	
	Number	Percent		Number	Percent
Fiction (of some kind)	39	74%	Fiction	22	39%
Nonfiction (of some kind)	11	21%	Free writing	11	20%
			Prompts	5	9%
Other	3	6%	Other	18	32%

Writer's workshop typically ends with a sharing time, often called Author's Chair, in which two or three students read their pieces aloud to the class (Harste, Short, & Burke, 1988, p. 46). However, Lensmire (1994) led me to rethink the benefits of this sharing time. He writes about the reluctance of certain students to read aloud their work to their classmates: "Although *almost no children* reported bad experiences in peer conferences, most *anticipated* bad experiences if they had conferences with certain children" (p. 82). Lensmire describes a specific sharing time that may have had negative consequences for a student writer named Rajesh:

If they tell Rajesh very politely, during sharing time, that they did not understand the meaning of parts of his story, what does that mean? What does it mean for Rajesh? What does it mean to me, as the teacher, especially if I do not know that Rajesh got pushed around at recess?...were their questions a subtle put down, voiced, of course, in appropriate language and tone, that made fun of Rajesh and his story? How do I know? (p. 83)

These comments about Author's Chair nagged at me. I remembered when I was the only person in the classroom raising my hand to respond to a student's story. I can remember other students raising their hands to offer feedback only to put down the writer with a snide "I don't really get it." Often the reader was an unpopular member of the class. I also had memories of myself reminding students to pay attention and be courteous to the writer during Author's Chair, only to feel that I had probably added to the child's discomfort with my comments, making it obvious to her and to everyone else that no one was listening to her. On the other hand, I also had memories of students being upset if we did not have time for Author's Chair or complaining that they had signed up days ago, asking, "When is it my turn?"

Lensmire calls for a rethinking of workshop structures such as Author's Chair and peer conferencing. Rosalyn, my daughter, loves to write, so I interviewed her about how she felt about sharing her writing. Her response was immediate and could have come directly from Lensmire's book.

Lee: Do you ever sign up for Author's Chair?

Rosalyn: No.

Lee: Why not?

Rosalyn: I don't like reading my writing to my class.

Lee: You don't? Why not?

Rosalyn: A lot of kids in my class like to share their stories because they are *very* funny. If your story is not funny, people aren't going to respond. They're just going to sit there. If you ask if they have any comments, they're just going to say no, basically. It feels weird, because if I have this story and I didn't want to make it funny, people are just sitting around and they're just looking around, you know?

How risky was it for students to share their writing with their classmates? Rosalyn's words prompted me to find out more about this issue through Question 4.

QUESTION 4: DO YOU LIKE TO SHARE YOUR WRITING WITH YOUR CLASS?

Response	Grade 3		Grade 6	
	Number	Percent	Number	Percent
Yes	25	47%	11	20%
No	22	42%	34	61%
Mixed	6	11%	11	20%

WHY OR WHY NOT?

Yes responses	Grade 3 (out of 25)	Yes responses	Grade 6 (out of 11)
I like to.	9	I like it.	5
I want people to know what I wrote.	6	I can get help.	2
It feels good to be complimented.	5	If the piece is good	2
They give me suggestions.	3	I like to see if they like it.	2
Other	2		

No responses	Grade 3 (out of 22)	No responses	Grade 6 (out of 34)
Shy/embarrassed/scared	19	Shy/embarrassed/scared	17
I don't like my stories.	3	I don't like it.	7
		My stories aren't always good.	4
		It's private.	3
		Other	3

The survey results mirror findings from Lensmire's study. If the "no" responses are combined with the "mixed" responses, I can see that reading aloud is scary or embarrassing for a majority of students. Of course, public speaking is difficult and can make all of us nervous, but perhaps the stress of Author's Chair might represent a significant obstacle for certain student writers. Although there always seemed to be someone willing to sit in the author's chair, I decided to rethink the workshop structure and replaced Author's Chair with Circle Check Out. At the end of writer's workshop, we would sit in a circle, and each writer could share an excerpt from his or her writing—sometimes a favorite sentence, or a lead, character description, or bits of dialogue. However, if a student did not want to share his or her writing, the student would be asked to give a progress report about what he or she had worked on that day during writer's workshop. Each day fewer students gave progress reports.

Concluding Thoughts

Researchers such as Lensmire, Kamler, Comber and Cormack, and Soo Hoo and Brown have critiqued writer's workshop as a place where writing is

- passive and consumerist,
- revered and treated as sacred even when it is sexist or violent, and
- a tool used by students to exclude or demean classmates.

My survey of over 100 students brought me to several conclusions: Writer's workshop should be a safe and supportive environment for all student writers. Fiction writing should be reintroduced to the workshop by using the fiction stories listed on the social-issue bibliography as examples of influential and powerful fiction. Writers should understand the potential social purposes of writing; an "eat-your-veggies-they're-good-for-you" approach to writing should be exchanged for a vision of writing as a tool for disrupting the commonplace and for taking social action.

CHAPTER 3

Writer's Workshop:
The Only Game in Town?

The Literacies and Differences course ended and so did a school year with an incredible group of third graders. In fall 2000, I started work on a master's thesis study about critical literacy in the writer's workshop. During the yearlong study, my classroom consisted of 20 third graders: 13 boys and 7 girls; 18 white; 1 Vietnamese American, adopted and brought to the United States at age 5; and 1 biracial student, with a white mother and a Chinese father. Because this was an inclusion classroom, 6 of the boys received special education services within the regular classroom setting. There was a wide range of abilities and interests within the group.

We started the year with writer's workshop that focused on personal narrative writing. As the school year progressed, we worked toward including more relevant writing in writer's workshop after discussing several social-issue texts in the bibliography (see Table 1 in chapter 1). Each day, I wrote field notes and collected writing samples from students. Students were interviewed at the end of the school year about their perceptions of the social-narrative stories they had written as well as about writing in general. Also, at the end of the school year, the students' stories were coded and analyzed for "story structure, themes, use of language, and representations of systems of power" (Heffernan & Lewison, 2003, p. 438).

Meeting the Student Authors

To learn more about the literate lives of my students, I asked them to bring from home personal artifacts, favorite books, and a favorite piece of writing. Many students nervously told me that they didn't have any writing to bring in. However, I reminded them that they had writing samples in their portfolios from previous years, which were kept at home. That evening, one mother e-mailed me to tell me that her son was worried about bringing a piece of writing to school because she wasn't sure they could find any. The next day, I told students not to worry about this part of the assignment—that bringing a piece of writing to class was optional. Although all 20 students brought in personal artifacts and 17 brought in favorite books, only 7 students accepted the invitation to bring in a favorite piece of writing. The writing pieces included

- an inquiry project (picture book) about knights written in first grade (Joshua)
- a pyramid poem written on a worksheet template (Rob)
- a report on zebras (Min)
- a summary of a picture book, *Two Bad Ants* (Van Allsburg, 1988) (Chase)
- a paragraph about baseball written as a result of my suggestion (Alex)
- a Pokémon story (John)
- a student picture book titled *The Magic Tree* (Peter)

Although most students had writing samples in their portfolios, they were reluctant to share them with classmates. This reluctance indicates support for Lensmire's (1994) findings about the potentially risky nature of sharing writing. It also supported my perception that many students did not have a strong emotional investment in the writing they created.

Writing With Passion

During the first week of school, I read to my class a chapter from *Ramona's World* (Cleary, 1999) in which the main character, Ramona, works on her first piece of writing in fourth grade. She writes passionately about her baby sister, describing her in clever detail. When Ramona is finished writing, she looks around at the other student writers, bored by their lists of favorite things or amused by the jokes they've written on their papers. I used this book chapter for my first writing minilesson. As a class, we compared Ramona's writing with the list-type writing of her classmates and discussed how Ramona's excitement about her baby sister comes through in an outpouring of descriptive writing. We talked about passions, and I asked the students to focus on and write about things they felt strongly about and knew a lot about. The following is an example of their chosen topics:

6 writers   sports

5 writers   pets

5 writers   Pokémon

1 writer   coins

1 writer   acting

1 writer   little sister

1 writer   television

The students' writing pieces were less than one page, clearly written, and very similar to pieces written by students in my previous classes. The pieces were shared, revised, edited, and published.

One student, Faith, wrote about her dog, Sammy, who had come to school on several occasions:

> My Dog Sammy would rather be on the road than on a leash. He is a skinny half beagle, half wiener dog. He chews up every single thing, including my shoes and my water bottle. He has short fur and is a fast runner.
>
> Sammy does not know his way around our surrounding neighborhood. One day he ran out of the door and ran about a half a mile, with me chasing him! One week later, I was away at a camp and he ran away again! Our neighbor Kerry and my mom ran about a mile trying to catch him. There was also a time when he slipped silently out of the basement door and followed a lady home. Luckily we got him back.
>
> Even though he is extremely fast, I still love him very much.

Rob wrote about his love of basketball in "NBA—Only Game in Town."

> Michael Jordan retired in 1998, but the NBA [National Basketball Association] is still awesome. I've liked the NBA for five years. My favorite teams are the Chicago Bulls and the Houston Rockets. My favorite players are Michael Jordan, Scottie Pippin and Kobe Bryant. They're really good at shooting. I don't mean to brag, but I'm a good shooter too.
>
> I know a lot about the NBA. There is an incredible amount of teams. There is an incredible amount of players, too. Only five men can play on a team.
>
> My favorite player is Michael Jordan. I like him because he's a very good player. Everybody calls him Jumpshot Jordan because he's good at jumpshots. I wish he wouldn't have retired. He was the greatest.
>
> You can probably tell I'm a really big fan of the NBA.

Although the students' enthusiasm for their topics is evident, the pieces and the writing assignment that prompted them reveal a psychological rather than a sociological response to writing. Writing about their passions did not help these writers to generate new understandings of their own lives or their social settings.

The Writing Carousel

During the first month of school, the writer's workshop progressed in a fairly typical way. The kids wrote daily. I presented minilessons on revising and editing, and the students became familiar with the processes of drafting, conferring, revising, editing, and publishing. As the students finished their drafts, they would meet with classmates at Author's Circle in which "authors read their pieces to the group for their responses and suggestions" (Short, Harste, & Burke, 1996, p. 106). The students also would use worksheets for revising and editing (see Figure 2).

One student, Rob, finished a piece about a trip to a haunted house. I met with him and suggested a few changes. He sat near me and wrote out his revisions, a few details, on sticky notes. As he popped the period onto his last sentence, he stood up and declared, "Now I'm going to write about my dog." Min and Faith also whipped through their writing, producing five to six pieces in less than a month—stories about their dogs, gymnastics, and sisters. I had the feeling that these students were rushing through the authoring cycle as if it were a high-speed carousel.

Although Faith and Rob were eager, confident writers, Gregory was not. He was a boy with many interests, but he struggled to get a few lines down on paper each day. Gregory's second-grade teacher had told me that in her class he had hated writing. One morning, Gregory was not writing anything but was sitting at his desk staring off into space. I had helped him with his first piece about baseball cards. I called him over and asked, "What do you want to write about next?"

"Monsters," he answered, without much excitement.

"OK, go for it," I told him. He walked away and came back in two minutes. On his paper he had written, "I like monsters. They are scary. They are big." I was not pleased. "This is all you wrote?" I asked, my tone dripping with incredulity.

"Well, that's all I can think of," he answered.

FIGURE 2. Author's Circle: Making Changes

1. Read your piece to yourself. If it all makes sense to you and you want to publish it, sign up for Author's Circle.

2. Meet with other authors at Author's Circle.

3. Read your piece to the other writers.

4. After you have finished reading, ask your audience,

> What did you hear? What stood out to you?

> Do you have any questions?

> Do you have any suggestions?

5. Listen to the other writers at Author's Circle.

6. On your own, revise in blue pen. Try to make 3 changes:

> Can you add any snapshots?

> Can you strengthen the lead and ending?

> Can you add a few power words?

7. Use the editing checklist to edit your work.

"Well if you don't know anything more than that about monsters, why do you want to write about them?"

"I know a lot about monsters!" he retorted defensively.

"Well, why don't you tell us what you know?" I replied. I was actually curious about why he didn't have more to say.

Gregory went to his desk and wrote three or four more sentences. "Frankenstein is a monster. Godzilla is a monster. Monsters can be big or small." Then he walked over to have a conference with a classmate about his piece.

Monster movies. Basketball stars. Pesky, but lovable, pets. Writer's workshop, in Yogi Berra's words, was like "déjà vu all over again."

Concluding Thoughts

The student writers in my class varied in their writing skill and in their enthusiasm, but at this point, I had failed to provide opportunities for my students to reflect on or rewrite their lives. They were writing what they knew about, but they weren't using writing to create new knowledge.

For my former students, the book *From Slave Ship to Freedom Road* (Lester, 1998) had stirred emotions and aroused their curiosities about the world. Could student writers create their own books that would have the same effect? Our rich conversations about social issues might be used as a resource—a springboard—for purposeful, provocative writing. In the next chapter, I outline procedures for eliciting conversational and written resources by working with social-issue texts using a six-session framework.

CHAPTER 4

Students as Text Workers

Early that same school year, I read *Crow Boy* (Yashima, 1976) to my third graders. Writers such as Taro Yashima, Eve Bunting, Julius Lester, and John Steptoe use the picture book genre to explore real-world issues with young readers. I was hopeful that student writers could learn from these authors and do the same with their writing.

Writing theorist Barbara Kamler (2001) believes students can benefit from being positioned as "text workers," people who can "work actively on the body of a text with intent to shape reader opinion" (p. 91).

Crow Boy is about a young boy who is ostracized and ignored for nearly his entire elementary school experience. Finally, in sixth grade, a teacher notices the boy and helps him to share his unique talent—imitating the sounds of crows—at the school talent show. After reading the book, I told my students, "When I read a book like this, I'm never really the same. It really makes me think about the way I treat people. Some books are like that."

A few days later, we read *Creativity* (Steptoe, 1997) in which the author interrogates the trappings of popular culture, telling how a newcomer to a sixth-grade class is teased because his clothes are "uncool." As a class, we discussed the similarities between *Crow Boy* and *Creativity* and gave our own examples of problems with being popular and fitting in. We talked about the need for friendship and reflected on the kind of classroom we wanted.

The themes in social-issue texts are complex and usually require several class sessions for reflective conversations to develop, but complicated and tricky issues have an important place in the elementary curriculum. Kohl (1995) believes that social-issue texts provide essential classroom experiences and allow us to imagine a new world:

> When there are no examples of stories for young people that fundamentally
> question the world as it is and dream it as it might be, resignation, defiance, or
> the quest for personal success become the only imaginable options unless the
> young have other sources for generating hope. (p. 63)

Also addressing this theme, Lensmire (1994) calls for teachers to work with "important texts" in the writer's workshop:

> Collective writing projects with important texts as "problems to be solved"—either in the production of certain genres of texts, or in the reading, interpretation, and criticism of texts—hold promise for our goals of helping children empower themselves in their reading and writing. (p. 155)

As a class, we spent four to six class sessions on each of the social-issue texts, generally following the procedure on the chart in Figure 3.

FIGURE 3.   Procedure for Extending Conversations About Social-Issue Texts

---

Session 1
The teacher reads aloud

Session 2
Pairs meet to discuss book and complete response sheet.
What's important to remember about this book? What surprised you?
What questions do you have?
Name a possible writing topic from your own life.

Session 3
Students meet in triads to discuss questions generated on the response sheets.
Groups monitor question list by placing a check mark next to questions that didn't generate much conversation and a plus sign or star next to questions that were discussed at length.

Session 4
The whole group discusses starred questions.

Session 5
The class finds a way to bookmark thinking about this book by choosing a picture to be represented on a "history trail."

Session 6
Students write one to two pages in notebooks about the writing topic chosen on the response sheet above.

From Vasquez, V. (with Muise, M.R., Adamson, S.C., Heffernan, L., Chiola-Nakai, D., & Shear, J. (2003). *Getting beyond "I like the book": Creating space for critical literacy in K–6 classrooms* (p. 37). Newark, DE: International Reading Association.

In the following sections, I outline the general procedures I use when working with social-issue texts.

Sessions 1 and 2: Reading and Responding

In the first session, I read the book aloud, rarely pausing to entertain student comments. Although I don't discourage students' opinions during the reading, I don't interrupt the story for conversation at this point. In session 2, I place students in random pairs to discuss the book and fill out a response sheet. Some of the prompts on the response sheet vary, but for the most part they ask students to do the following:

- Write a question about this book.
- Write one thing that's important about this book.
- Write down something that surprised you.
- Write down a topic from your own life that connects in some way to this book.

Other possible prompts for the response sheet include

- Tell whose voice was heard in this book. Tell whose voice was not heard.
- Tell who had the most power in this text. Tell who had the least.
- Choose two characters with different perspectives and write what they would say to each other if they could meet in real life.
- Identify the ideal reader of this text. (Who should read this book?)
- Is this text realistic? Tell why or why not.
- Is there anything you doubt about this text? Explain.

The response sheet is meant as a conversational device. Partners do not need to have the same answers or responses in each box. The main focus is on generating discussion about the text. On the response sheets, Gregory chose to write about being small (see Figure 4a), while Faith chose to focus on her memory of being a kindergartner who was so afraid of school that she would not eat her lunch (see Figure 4b).

FIGURE 4a.   Response to *Crow Boy*: Gregory

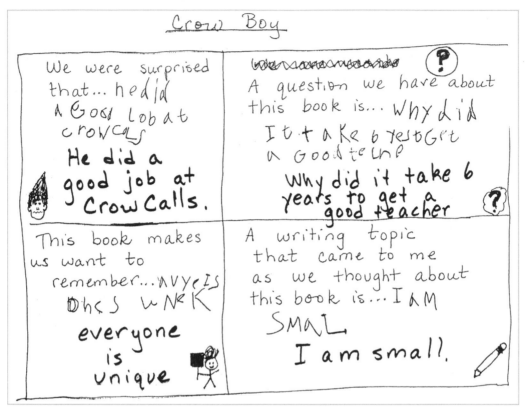

Session 3: Triangle Talk

To initiate triangle talk, I handed out typed questions from the response sheet to randomly selected groups of three students. (I use ice cream sticks with names on them for grouping.) Within the groups, students discuss and critique the questions according to the quality of discussion the question generated. Students put a check mark next to a question that has an obvious answer or that does not merit much discussion and put a plus sign or a star next to a question that generates lengthier, more interesting talk. Some groups move through all the questions on the list while other groups linger over a few. I spend about 15 to 20 minutes on triangle talk. (See Figure 5 for response sheet for *Crow Boy*.)

FIGURE 4b. Response to *Crow Boy:* Faith

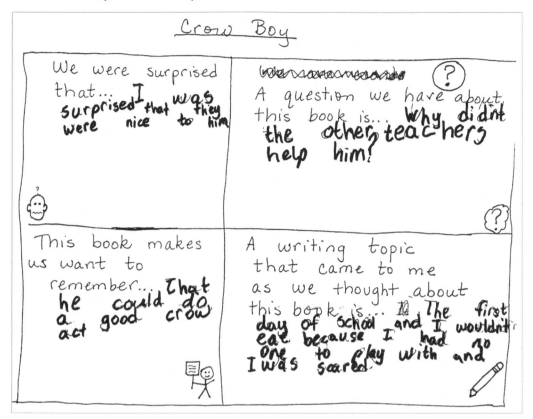

Crow Boy

We were surprised that... I surprised that was they were nice to him

A question we have about this book is... Why didnt the other teachers help him! (?)

This book makes us want to remember... That he could do a act good crow

A writing topic that came to me as we thought about this book is... The first day of school and I wouldnt eat because I had no one to play with and I was scared

Sessions 4 and 5: Whole-Group Talk and History Trail

To prepare for whole-group talk, I circulate, participate, and take notes while students, in groups of two or three, discuss the questions generated from the response sheets. After discussing the book in groups, the class comes together as a whole group to review the questions. These conversations tend to be lively and emotional. Quieter students speak out more frequently, perhaps, because the increased time and the smaller group participation have allowed their ideas to percolate more fully. After this session, we meet again and picture walk through the book with the intention of choosing a picture that most typifies the ideas from our conversations (see Figure 6).

FIGURE 5. Response Sheet for *Crow Boy*

Name _____ Date _____

Why did people think Crow Boy was stupid?

Why did Crow Boy get the nickname Chibi?

Where did the zebra grass come from?

How did Crow Boy get through all the grades if he could not learn anything?

Why didn't Crow Boy say "hi" in the first place?

How did Crow Boy make the crow sound?

Is the author a man or woman?

Why did people make fun of Crow Boy when he was only short?

What is important about this book?

_____ Crow Boy was accepted at the end.

_____ It shows not to make fun of people.

_____ People who are picked on can surprise you.

_____ It's important to watch nature and learn about it.

_____ The talent show showed everyone what Crow Boy could do.

_____ Even though some people have their feelings hurt, they can still live a good life.

FIGURE 6.   Page From *Voices in the Park*

Girls and Boys Can Play Together

These pictures and captions are placed on a large bulletin board that we call our "history trail" (see Harste & Vasquez, 1998, p. 273). The physical representation of key conversations in classroom life later becomes a resource for student writers.

Session 6: Notebook Writing

At first, students found it difficult to think of writing topics that connected to their own lives even after listening to the social-issue texts, so I demonstrated with a read-aloud book. After reading portions of *Ramona's World* (Cleary, 1999), I would stop at certain points and say, "Can anyone think of a topic that this chapter makes them want to write about?" At first, silent stares were the typical responses; therefore, I shared my own ideas: "This chapter makes me think about writing about something that happened to me once. One time I had to go to a meeting with some people I didn't know, and I was really very nervous about it. So I may write about that feeling I have around new people." Although these personal connections did not stand out as truly sociological in nature, I forged ahead with this approach, thinking that these personal pieces might lead to bigger topics when gathered together.

Both *Crow Boy* and *Creativity* deal with schoolchildren being ostracized because they are different from their peers in some way. Most students focused on the topics of "teasing" and "differences" in their connecting writing (see Figure 7a and Figure 7b). Although many students wrote about specific incidents of being teased, usually at school, these topics, retellings of some uncomfortable, if not outright painful experiences, are not typical of self-selected topics in a third-grade writer's workshop. Although students recalled individual incidents, patterns in the notebook entries emerged. Students had been teased about their names, clothing, hair, abilities in sports, and for being new at school. As they listened to one another read aloud their pieces, they recognized and discussed the incongruity between school guidelines—which included trust, caring, and friendship—and the exclusion and ridicule that pervades school culture. At the same time, the power of the connections of shared experiences became common ground for the writers in this classroom.

FIGURE 7a. Student's Writing Sample: Teasing

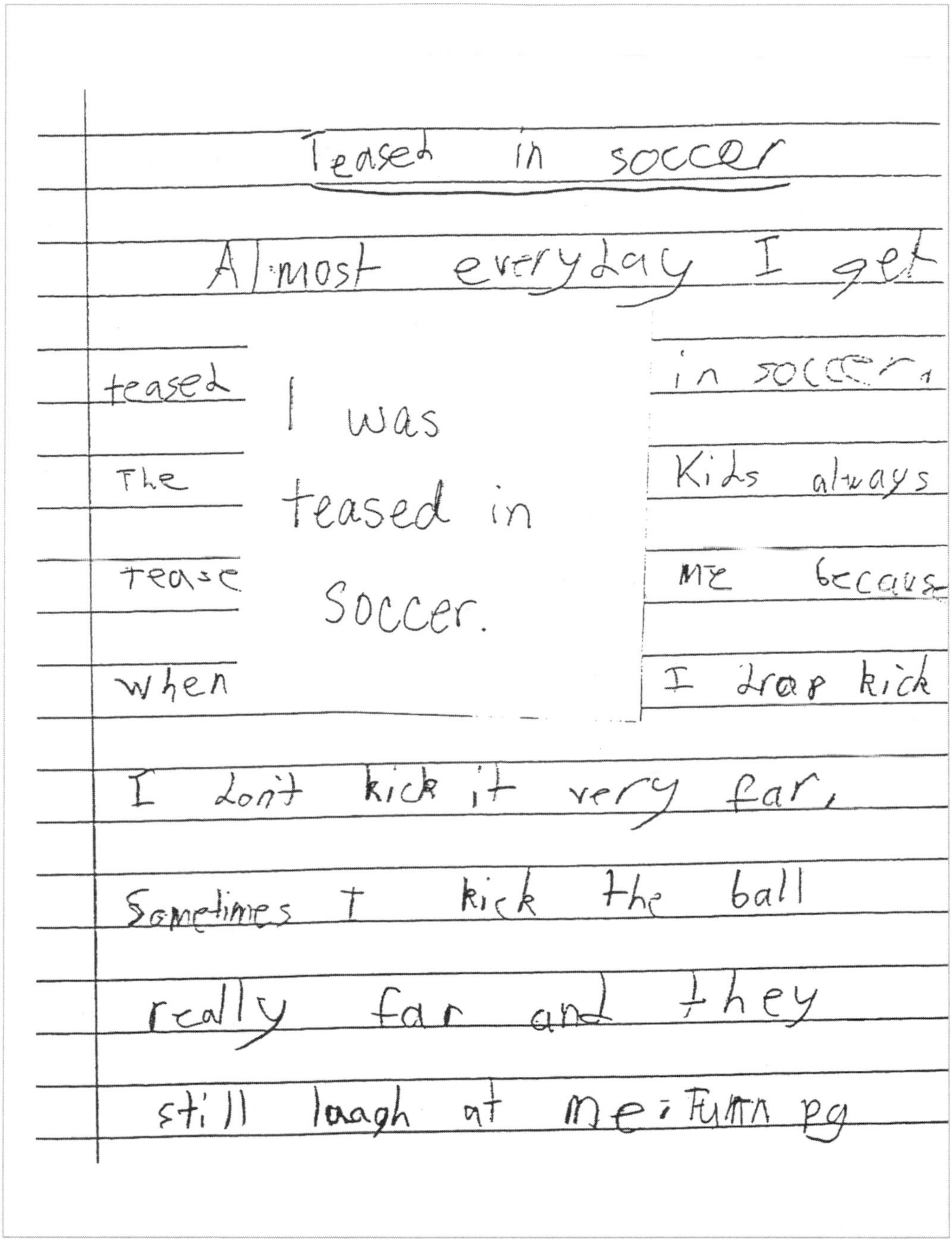

Teased in soccer

Almost everyday I get

teased

The

teasc

when

in soccer

Kids always

me becaus

I drop kick

I was

teased in

soccer.

I don't kick it very far.

Sometimes I kick the ball

really far and they

still laugh at me. Turn pg

FIGURE 7b.   Student's Writing Sample: Differences

My Face

writing topic

People make fun
of my face Sometimes.

Once a while people

make fun of my face.

Just because its a little

Different, Like at recess

he said that my

face Looks Like a Ded

racoon face. When he said

that it harted my

feelings. It is not nice

to make fun of people's

face. Because how would

you like to be called

names? I bet that you

Concluding Thoughts

The social-issue texts became a tool for exploring our connections to one another. My work with these texts has since evolved and now includes not only picture books but news articles, advertisements, videos, and school experiences and conversations. The three most important classroom resources for student writers are

1. Social-issue texts such as *Crow Boy*, *Creativity*, and *Voices in the Park*

2. Classroom conversations

3. Entries in writer's notebooks

The conversations about the social-issue texts, which occurred over many class sessions, pulled the students together as a community. These conversations ended up being pivotal events in our classroom. The students later used key ideas from all these resources in their own social-narrative picture books.

CHAPTER 5

Talker's Workshop: Expanding Writing Resources to Include Social Themes

In the middle of a conversation about a book, a student, Danny, interrupted to say, "We really should call this 'talker's workshop' because we spend a way lot of time talking in this class."

Each school year, with different groups of students, conversations about texts vary and different themes are highlighted. In this first year of working with social narratives, racism became a key classroom theme because of the risk-taking of the two Asian American students. We also had conversations about gender differences, economic differences, popularity, the Pokémon craze, materialism, and the displacement of U.S. jobs to Mexico.

Racism: People Make Fun of My Face

In response to *Crow Boy*, students John and Min wrote about racist incidents that had occurred at our school. Min, Vietnamese American, wrote on her response sheet, "People make fun of my face sometimes." John, a biracial student, wrote, "Kids make fun of me just because I'm part Chinese."

Athough I had taught three Asian American students the previous year and had discussed over 20 social-issue texts with them, they had never brought up personal experiences of racism. This made me wonder if adding the writing dimension to the project had led to a more comfortable forum for students to discuss their lives. Discussing these incidents in a room full of classmates could have been scary for my students from the previous school year. This year, however, Min and John could use writing to mediate and present their experiences to classmates.

In *Why Are All the Black Kids Sitting Together in the Cafeteria?* Tatum (1997) writes about this keeping-it-to-yourself phenomenon:

> In large groups, I hcsitate to ask the participants to reveal their (race-related) memories to a crowd of strangers, but I ask instead what emotions are attached to the memories.... Too often the stories are painful ones. Then I ask,

"Did you talk to anyone about what happened? Did you tell anyone how you felt?" It is always surprising to me to see how many people will say that they never discussed clearly emotional experiences with anyone. (pp. 31–32)

As students began writing personal connections to *Crow Boy* in their notebooks, John walked up to me and asked, "Is it OK if I write about this, because it really happened?" He pointed to his response sheet on which he had written, "People teased me because I'm half Chinese."

I told him, "Yes, I think that's a very important topic. Go for it." He went back to his desk. Devra, sitting next to John, must have read his title because she walked up to me soon after and said, "John's sticky-note makes me want to change mine. I was going to write about people making fun of my pants one day, but I want to write about being Jewish. Is that OK to change my topic?"

"Sounds good to me," I told her. When we gathered at the rug to sit in a circle and share our notebook entries, John chose not to share when his turn came. Min, however, read the following piece to the class:

Once in awhile people make fun of my face. Just because it's a little different. Like at recess, one kid said that my face looks like a dead raccoon's face. When he said that it hurted my feelings. It is not nice to make fun of people's face. Because how would you like to be called names? I bet that you wouldn't feel good. And it isn't my fault that I was born different.

The students were silent when Min finished reading. The ever-dramatic Devra yelled out, "But Min's beautiful!" John raised his hand and said he would also like to read his piece, which he read to the class:

In kindergarten, we had a paper where we had to write where your parents are from. I sent in that my dad was Chinese, and my mom was Spanish, German, English and French. Everyone looked at my paper and it said my dad was Chinese and my mom was a lot of things, that meant I was Chinese, English, German, etc.... And they made fun of me because I was part a lot of things.

Race would come up again, many times, as we read other social-issue texts.

Voices in the Park (Browne, 1998) explores class issues. The story is about a mother who does not want her child to play with another child at the park, and it is told through four different voices: (1) a wealthy mother, (2) her son, (3) an unemployed father, and (4) his daughter. Responding to *Voices in the Park*, Min surprised me with her comment, "I think the mother doesn't like Smudge because she's darker!" Min had connected the racism she had experienced on the playground with the experience of the girl character in the book, who actually was no different than the boy character in terms of skin color.

Working with social-issue texts allowed Min and John to write and talk about their experiences with racism. Through their brave sharing of their experiences, we all were educated about the difficulties of being in a minority group in a mostly white school. Seven students would later write about racism as a theme in their own picture books.

Sexism: Girls Rule, Boys Drool

After we read *Voices in the Park*, I asked students about the boy character's statement about meeting a playmate at the park, "Unfortunately, she was a girl." The students talked about being teased for having friends of the opposite gender. Most of the students were appalled at the snootiness of the mother. Paul wrote on his response sheet, "LET KIDS PLAY WITH KIDS!"

I began taking on the role of activist in the classroom. When we read about racism or sexism in social-issue texts or the newspaper, I would remind the students, "Well we know this is something that happens right here at our own school. It happened to kids in our own class" or "Remember when I read *Voices in the Park* and we talked about boys and girls being teased for being friends? Today, I'm going to read another book that tells us more about that." Rather than let these kind of incidents slip away unnoticed, I would bring them up repeatedly, as I myself noticed connections to our earlier conversations.

My critical stance made me more aware of opportunities for discussing power issues with the students. One day, as Gregory began a piece of writing with "Girls are dumb. Girls are stupid," I was surprised, considering the conversations we had been having since school began. I thought of Lensmire's (1994) comment that there are "times when children's writing should be questioned—not followed" (p. 16). I said to Gregory, "You know this seems kind of rude to me. We have talked about sexism before and this seems sexist. When you write bad things about a whole group of people, it's not very fair."

Meanwhile, Drew stopped writing, looked up at me, and in a tentative voice said, "Well, I've heard teachers say, 'Girls rule—boys drool' and I didn't like *that* too much."

I answered, "I wouldn't like that either. I have a daughter and a son, and I think they're both wonderful. Even joking statements like that can keep people apart." Three students would later write about gender issues as a theme in their own picture books.

Consumerism: The Pokémon Phenomenon

Current events and popular trends also came up during our conversations. In fall of the school year, the kids were rabid about Pokémon, and the cards were banned at school. Because my own son was a Pokémon fan, I remained sheepishly quiet during these conversations. I talked to my class one day about the craze: "You know, my little boy collects the cards, and I'm starting to think that it's kind of a rip-off. I buy him these booster packs, and he hardly gets any new cards. Then he's really disappointed."

Rob answered, "Yeah, they make you buy more and more cards."

Regina added, "I know. I bought three packs last week, and I didn't even get a holo [holographic card]."

Drew joined in, "I know. I like the cards, but it's kind of stupid how you have to spend so much money to get any good cards. But you know, they said they were going to stop making Beanie Babies, and I think that's just to make more money, too."

The students were at ease talking about these fads, calmly acknowledging that they were allowing themselves to be ripped off. Of course, they probably weren't spending their own money on the cards, so they probably had limited pity for the plight of their parents, but they did have an awareness of how the Pokémon "system" seemed to work. They weren't ignorant participants. Two students later explored the negative aspects of Pokémon mania in their picture books.

Capitalism: Jobs Go to Mexico

In our town, one large employer announced during the year that it would cut the local workforce by eliminating 1,400 jobs and moving the jobs to Mexico. Alex brought this current event to morning meeting one day. We discussed the different standards of living in Bloomington, Indiana, and Mexico. The students wanted to know why Mexican workers would work for less money. I read to the students *Going Home* (Bunting, 1996), which is a book about a

Mexican family living in California. The family drives back to their village in Mexico for a holiday visit with extended family, and the children realize all that their parents have given up in order to provide them with future economic and academic opportunities. The book not only gave us a chance to compare the economic situations in Mexico and California, but it also brought to light many positive aspects of living in Mexico.

The theme of the book is "opportunities." While working on research projects about our town, several students worked on skits about the company's decision to move jobs to Mexico, mentioning the importance of opportunities. Three boys wrote and read an intercom announcement to tell the rest of the school about this issue.

During one classroom talk about *Going Home*, John surprised me: "This book is really about secrets, because the kids really don't know about the parents and what they're really like." We talked about family secrets for a while and why parents might move their family to a new place. Seven students chose the theme of moving to a new culture for economic opportunities for their picture books.

Playground Politics: Name Calling at Recess

One conversation stood out from the others when we discussed *Flying Solo* (Fletcher, 1998), a book about a class of sixth graders who take control of their classroom when the teacher is absent and no substitute arrives to replace him. As we talked about the way one character was put down because of her weight, Joshua looked up from his desk and said, "People call me 'fat' at recess."

Alex, who always had a smile on his face, looked troubled and said quietly, "They call me that too."

I responded, "That's horrible."

John added, "When I'm playing soccer, two kids in the other third grade chase me and yell 'Chinese Boy!' while I'm trying to kick the ball."

I said, "You mean this happened a while ago?" I was thinking about John's stories about kindergarten.

He said, "No, it happens almost every day."

I was stunned. I looked at the other students, "Have you ever heard anyone call John 'Chinese Boy'?" Many students nodded silently.

After a few more students shared, Chase, who has a neurological disorder, broke in, "Well, people make fun of me because I wave my hands around a lot." Then he began to cry, which was not uncommon for him. I noticed Faith sinking her head down onto her arms on her desk.

Gregory, always very quiet during class discussions, blurted out, "Well, people call me 'short' all the time."

Paul said, "I didn't know you cared about that. We just do it to be funny."

Gregory answered him, "Well, sometimes it bugs me."

Peter approached me. "What are we talking about right now?" he asked quietly in my ear.

"We're talking about people hurting other people's feelings."

"Yes, that happened to me! Last year at recess, they called me 'Screwed-up-face boy'!" he announced to everyone.

Steven yelled out, "I was there! I heard them say that to Peter."

We talked more about events at recess. Everyone had a story to tell about being teased or hurt, being ignored by the spread-too-thin recess supervisors, or having nothing to do or no one to play with. I agreed to go out and periodically supervise their soccer games. We also talked about helping one another when someone is teased or called names. These were not solutions but small attempts to do *something*. The class as a whole had exposed the world of "playground hell" that was uniquely theirs. Recess or playground politics would appear as themes in 16 of 19 picture books written by students.

Concluding Thoughts

Conversations that involve the injustices experienced by students can be tricky for teachers. Upon hearing about some of the troubling talk in my classroom, a colleague said, "Well, a lot of this kind of teasing can be playful." Another friend who works with children outside of a school setting told me, "Don't get too worked up about it. We all survive childhood, Lee." The comments that the students shared did worry me, though. As teachers, how do we know when teasing is playful and when it's not? Did school have to be a place that students "survived"?

Throughout the conversations we had over the course of the school year, the students revealed a depth of feeling in their talk that seemed absent from the discussions in past years. At my school, we are, for the most part, middle class, comfortable suburbanites. Despite privileged backgrounds, the students showed that they were not self-absorbed or uncaring when confronted with the problems of others. Rather, they wanted to talk about these big issues because they had unanswered and troubling questions and appreciated having opportunities to focus on difficult and troubling social problems. As Freire (1998) writes, schools should not "dichotomize emotion and cognition" (p. 3). Coles (1998) also calls for teachers to bring literacy and emotions together in classrooms, stating that "cognition, emotions, and learning do not 'co-vary'— rather, they interact" (pp. 78–79).

The emotional aspect of our conversations contributed to the quality of the social-narrative writing that the students ultimately produced. The connections students made to the books we read contained personal insights and peculiarities and an authenticity that made for intriguing talk and, potentially, for interesting reading. At first, I had worried that the project would be too personal, and perhaps more psychological than sociological, with the students responding with specific, individual connections and concerns. What the students found was that they weren't the only ones who had had difficulty with teasing or bullying—that they weren't solitary victims. They discovered that school can be an oppressive place for different people for different reasons. They also acknowledged that sometimes they themselves had teased and hurt others. All the students investigated the personal and the political issues of school in their stories.

CHAPTER 6

Theme Search: First Steps Toward Writing Social Narratives

To get students thinking about using thematic purpose in their writing, I began writer's workshop one day by revisiting *Crow Boy* (Yashima, 1976). As the students sat on the rug in front of me, I sat next to our chart stand, held up the book, and said, "When Taro Yashima wrote this book, I think he wanted us to think about some pretty big ideas and questions. When I read this book, I thought about what kind of teacher I want to be. Big ideas in books are often called *themes*. What themes or big ideas come to mind when you think about *Crow Boy*?"

Amelia's hand shot up. "I think he wanted us to think about getting along with everyone, even different people."

On a chart, I wrote "Accepting People" and "Accepting Differences." I asked the students to come up with others. "Finding out what's special about someone," Joshua shouted out.

Rob spoke up, "Not to tease someone."

I added "Special Talents" and "Teasing" to the chart. Devra said, "Maybe someone teased him when he was a kid, so he wanted to write a book about that so other people wouldn't do that."

"I think you could be right," I said. "Because that's what a lot of writers do. They write about things that confuse them or bother them. They try to figure these things out when they write. Last quarter, we wrote pieces about things that interested us—trips we had taken, things we collect, friends we have. Those pieces were great and they helped us to learn more about each other. This quarter, though, I'd like to see if we can explore some themes or questions in our writing in the way Yashima did with *Crow Boy*." We also identified the themes in all the books we read together and added them to the list on the chart (see Table 2).

TABLE 2.   Themes in the Books Read Together

Books	Themes
Crow Boy (Yashima, 1976)	Accepting people Accepting differences Special talents Teasing Caring about others
Creativity (Steptoe, 1997)	Friendship Why are clothes so important? We're all from different backgrounds and races.
Voices in the Park (Browne, 1998)	Money differences (economics) Friendship Let kids play with kids. Excluding people Judging people
Going Home (Bunting, 1996)	Opportunities Money differences (economics) Secrets in families Why make sacrifices for education?
Flying Solo (Fletcher, 1998)	Teacher authority Kid power Teasing Secrets
Angel Child, Dragon Child (Surat, 1989)	Accepting differences Getting to know people Being apart from your family Taking action
Nobody Owns the Sky (Lindbergh, 1999)	Sexism/racism Are there different opportunities in different countries? Equal rights
Wilma Unlimited: How Wilma Rudolph Became the World's Fastest Woman (Krull, 1996)	Physical disabilities Sexism/racism Desegregation

Themes From Notebook Entries

Students responded regularly to social-issue texts by writing in their notebooks. I photocopied all the notebook entries that connected to the social-issue texts, and as I looked through them, I noted that almost all the students had produced some very thoughtful writing. Three students, however, had simply summarized the plots of the social-issue texts, which would end up being of little help when writing their picture books. I knew that I needed to be clearer about using the texts to write about personal connections when we wrote future notebook entries. Most students, however, had accumulated a packet of about eight personal life events.

I, too, had a packet of pieces to use as a model for a lesson on identifying themes. Flipping through the pages, I talked about my writing to the class:

> Here's a piece about pressuring my kid to buy a Pokémon backpack because I didn't want him to be teased at school. He wanted a backpack that I considered to be for preschoolers. The theme for that piece could be "popularity" or "parenting mistakes." I'm probably going to use that in my picture book because that memory still really bothers me. Here's a piece about kids at a camp I taught at once who didn't mix because they were from different schools. That theme could be "teasing" or "excluding." Here's a piece about everyone always being shocked that my husband cooks dinner every night. That theme could be "women's work" or something about the roles of men and women. I could probably use that one, too, in my book. Look through your own packets and see which themes you can identify in your writing. Write your themes in the top margins of your entries. Pick at least three notebook entries that you might use for your own picture book.

The demonstration was successful. The students were anxious to look for themes in their packets. A few students needed help, but most students happily sifted through their entries, writing down themes. Devra brought her packet to me and remarked, "I think this one about being Jewish is stronger than this other one about students laughing at my army pants. What do you think?" I told her they were both strong and she should decide.

Drew came up to me and said, "These two tie together. The dad is into sports and the student is being teased on the soccer field. My book could be about secrets because maybe the student doesn't want to tell the dad." His comment reminded me of our conversation about secrets in *Going Home* (Bunting, 1996).

Rose, who had basically written summaries in reaction to the social-issue texts, came up to me and said, "I want to write about being little, but it's not in my packet." Rose is a very short girl who is extremely quiet. I asked, "Did you get this idea when Gregory talked about being short?" She confirmed my guess. I told her she could still focus on that theme but that she should look through her packet to find a piece that could tie into a story about being small. She went back to her desk and began reading through her packet again.

Rob and Danny wanted help with identifying themes. Danny said, "I might want to write about friendship or maybe fear of the dark."

Rob said, "I know my title. It's going to be 'Hey Popular Kid! It's Opposite Day' but I'm not sure why he's popular." We talked about what makes kids popular at our school, including sports ability and large collections of Pokémon cards.

Joshua walked around the classroom reading other students' pieces. He kept saying, "These pieces are great! I can't stop reading them." I worried that this might be an attempt to avoid his own work, but I let him continue. It was nice to have someone in the class so appreciative of other students' writing.

A few other students had problems starting, but overall I felt the session had been successful. The students were poring over their pieces in a way that, at the time, seemed quite literary to me. They weren't rushing. They read through them all, sharing favorite pieces with one another, placing stickers next to examples of strong writing, and jotting down themes in the margins.

Picture Book Proposals

The following day, students met with partners to talk about their themes and to read the pieces they were considering for inclusion in their picture books. They filled out a Picture Book Project form for their books (see Figure 8).

When we met back on the rug, I asked the students to share their themes. As I began to write on chart paper, I said, "We want our books to really make people..."

"Change!" Devra burst in.

This seemed a bit too grand or ambitious, so I told her, "Well, we hope to make people *think* about some of the things that we've been talking about."

FIGURE 8.   Picture Book Project

Purpose: We've read the following powerful books that have big themes. We've had amazing conversations about our own connections. Now it's time to write a picture book that will make people in and out of school think and talk about "Differences" and fairness.

> *Creativity* (Steptoe, 1997)
> *Crow Boy* (Yashima, 1976)
> *Flying Solo* (Fletcher, 1998)
> *Nobody Owns the Sky* (Lindbergh, 1999)
> *Ramona's World* (Cleary, 1999)
> *Voices in the Park* (Browne, 1998)

Directions: Use your notebook entries to get started.

Look through your notebook entries. Do any pieces stand out to you?

Place a sticker next to any sections that seem especially interesting and original.

If you have explored any big themes in your writing, write them at the top of your notebook page.

How can you include your notebook entries in a picture book that will make readers have big conversations?

Share your pieces with your learning partner.

Fill in the following proposal form.

PICTURE BOOK PROPOSAL

I want to write about the theme _____.

I will use _____ notebook entries from my packet.

My book will be   fiction   nonfiction.   (circle one)

As the students talked, I wrote the themes on chart paper. When almost everyone had shared, I told the students that the list was a collection of serious issues they could draw from when planning their own books and "If kids at our school read your books, they may really think about the problems we've been having with teasing and name calling."

Topics Versus Themes

I could have quit while I was ahead, but I asked Andrew to share his theme. He looked at me and said matter of factly, "I'm going to write about the time I got stitches."

This was a small dilemma for me. I hesitated, wondering how forceful I wanted to be with my new focus on themes. I had always considered choice to be an essential condition of learning. At that moment, though, I felt that if I didn't push all students to choose themes over topics, the students might bail out, retreating to the record-keeper kind of writing of past workshops. I decided to press my point. "What theme will you be exploring in your story about getting stitches, Andrew?"

"I don't know."

"Do you want to include your piece about kids being mean out on the soccer field to your stitches story?"

"No. That's not how it happened."

"I know. But remember that we're trying to write books that really make people think about big ideas. So keep thinking about themes tonight when you're at home, OK?"

Frances broke into our conversation, "I have an idea for Andrew. He could write about some of the violence that has been happening on the soccer field and that could lead to someone getting stitches and then they could figure out that they shouldn't be so rough."

This caused the class to erupt with more soccer field horror stories. Joshua yelled out, "I'm writing about soccer, too!"

The soccer field was a key site for the social lives of these third graders. Frances and Joshua and others in the class had developed some awareness that their social experiences could be explored through writing topics.

Concluding Thoughts

The students jumped into theme work, reading published texts and their own notebook entries in an attempt to identify underlying issues or purposes. Andrew's resistance, or reluctance, to focus on a theme brought to mind the questions Soo Hoo and Brown (1994) asked about a teacher's role in guiding students to write about social issues—"Will a social agenda emerge naturally in writing or does the teacher have to do something?" (p. 102). As a teacher, I had to face the fact that I did have to *do something* if students were to see themselves as purposeful and powerful writers. I had to take an active role in the types of writing that occurred during writer's workshop. A push for thematic purpose in the workshop is more than an arbitrary restriction of choice—it is a step toward creating a space in which student writers use writing as a tool for exploring and generating social awareness.

CHAPTER 7

Revising Writer's Workshop

Writer's workshop had an energetic, busy quality to it as the students worked on their picture books. Their rough drafts took several weeks to complete. Writing longer pieces helped students to develop ideas in more depth. With everyone involved in this major writing project, I was able to be a different kind of writing teacher than I had been in the past. My teaching methods and the workshop itself began to change. Following are some of the changes I made to the workshop:

- using social-issue texts as a source for minilessons
- revising drafts through word-processing procedures
- replacing Author's Chair with Circle Check Out

These revisions to the workshop format improved the quality of student writing and enhanced the general atmosphere in the classroom as students became writing resources for one another.

Learning From Authors

Fiction had always been my least favorite genre for students to write. But because 18 of 20 students planned to write a fiction story, I knew I would have to improve my teaching skills in this area. Therefore, I planned minilessons using the social-issue texts as models of quality, purposeful fiction writing. I also drew from the history trail texts (see chapter 4) because they had become established reference material. Students were accountable for incorporating minilesson concepts into their stories and sharing evidence of this at the workshop's conclusion during Circle Check Out.

Starting With Storyboards

After students selected one or two themes to explore in their picture books, we created storyboards to plan the stories. The storyboards consisted of six sticky notes placed on a piece of notebook paper, each note containing a caption and sketch of a main event in the story (see Figure 9). Each sticky note idea had to be stretched into a single page of text, but students were required to skip lines. With storyboards in hand, students talked through their stories with partners and then with me before they began writing.

As the students got further into writing their stories, the stories frequently deviated from the storyboards. As the stories took different turns, students would rework their storyboards—easily removing and replacing the sticky notes—in order to reorganize the plots. Students consulted their storyboards daily.

Minilessons: The Nuts and Bolts of Writing

Whenever I taught a minilesson, I used some snippet of text from the history trail texts to call attention to elements of the writing craft. Students knew that they would be asked to demonstrate their use of concepts presented in minilessons at Circle Check Out at the end of the workshop.

Minilesson: Using Power Words

In *Crow Boy* (Yashima, 1976), the main character, Chibi, is described as a "forlorn little tagalong" (n.p.). The students and I talked about the powerful images and inferences evoked by these words. We then looked through history trail texts to gather other "power words" that were especially creative or evocative. These words were written on "word tickets" (Wooldridge, 1996, p. 14) by students who then went around the room comparing tickets with classmates and gathering new words on new tickets. I asked students to write down classmates' power words that they might find particularly useful in their stories.

Minilesson: Time Shifts

During writing, many students asked questions such as, How do you get to dinnertime if you don't want to put the whole day in? and I want the school year to be over now. How can I do that? Using a minilesson about time shifts (Lane, 1993), we looked at the ways in which the author controlled time in *Crow Boy*. The students loved the sentence "And so, day by day, five years went by, and we were in the sixth grade, the last class in school" (n.p.).

FIGURE 9.   Sample of Storyboard

We looked in other books for examples of authors controlling time and created a list of terms that could be used to move the action ahead, such as *the next day*, *months passed*, and *the day finally arrived*. At Circle Check Out, I asked students to share how much time would pass in their stories. Some stories took place over one day, while others spanned an entire school year.

Minilesson: Snapshot Strategy

Quite a few students described characters by writing things such as "Grace is 9. She has red hair. She has blue eyes. She wears a red jacket." Because students were having trouble with descriptive writing, I used passages from the social-issue texts to give examples of more descriptive writing. Using the "snapshot" strategy (Lane, 1993, p. 32), we matched showing statements to telling statements on the Snapshots worksheet (see Figure 10).

At Circle Check Out, each student shared a snapshot. Students who finished early were also required to read over their story and add snapshots on sticky notes to three pages of text in order to further support their ideas.

Minilesson: Paragraphing

Although the students' stories were getting to be four or five pages long, they all were one paragraph. As we looked over the text of *Crow Boy*, we counted the sentences in each paragraph. Then, we talked about why the author may have split up the story as he did. During the writing session, two boys said they wanted to look at the way Steptoe (1997) used paragraphs in *Creativity*. As I worked with another student, Drew interrupted me, shouting, "In *Creativity*, his paragraphs have about 5 or 6 sentences in them, but mine have about 19 sentences in them."

"Yeah, I've noticed that," I responded, attempting to be casual about the whole thing. I had talked about paragraphing dozens of times that year, but I continued calmly, "Can you think of a way to break up the text a bit and give your reader some resting places?" I had worked hard on minilessons and, in the past, had used literature as their main source, but these lessons were different because the students, as a group, had strong emotional ties to these books—and they knew them very well. I, too, felt an attachment to these books, and I turned to them again and again to discover how the authors embedded their messages in the texts.

FIGURE 10.   Snapshots Worksheet: Show, Don't Tell

Purpose: We've read the following books in which authors have described scenes using vivid detail. They *show* us what is happening, rather than *tell* us. How do the snapshots help readers to see pictures in their minds?

> *Angel Child, Dragon Child* (Surat, 1989)
> *Crow Boy* (Yashima, 1976)
> *Going Home* (Bunting, 1996)
> *Wilma Unlimited* (Krull, 1996)
> *Women of Hope* (Hansen, 1998)

Directions: Do any of the following passages create a picture in your mind as you read? Match each passage with one of the books above.

1. He crinkled his paper and snapped the pencil in two. He hid his head in his arms.

2. My fingers danced on the desktop while I waited for the bell. When it rang, I rushed out the door. Outside, snowflakes left wet kisses on my cheeks.

3. During playground games she could only sit on the sidelines, twitchy with impatience. She studied the other kids for hours—memorizing moves, watching the ball zoom through the rim of the bushel basket they used as a hoop.

4. The heat in the strawberry fields. The sun pushing down between the rows of tomatoes. The little flies biting our faces.

5. Even when it rained or stormed he still came trudging along, wrapped in a raincoat made from dried zebra grass.

6. There was a former slave who lived alone. Mama always sent us over there to check up on him. Every Sunday, we shared our dessert with him.

Match the *showing* statement above with the *telling* statement below.

___ We always helped out other people.
___ I wanted to go home.
___ Farm work is really hard.
___ She wanted to play with the others.
___ One time he walked in the rain.
___ The boy was sad.

Becoming an Editor: Forming Revision Partnerships

I told my students about hearing Avi, one of my favorite authors, speak at a conference. I exuberantly proclaimed, "You know how many times Avi rewrites his books? Forty or fifty times! We're going to work and work on our stories until they're as powerful as they can be!"

In the past, I had always handed back rough drafts attached to a response sheet containing positive comments and one or two revision suggestions. Then, I would meet with students and have them attempt to fix one or two parts of their piece. At first, when Rose and Faith turned in their rough drafts to read, I panicked. I had wanted these stories to be phenomenal, but they weren't that great: Rose's story was skeletal, and Faith's was confusing. I eventually calmed down and figured out a way to help these students revise. Two things helped me: (1) checking for thematic clarity and (2) implementing word processing for revisions.

Checking for Thematic Clarity

As I read through Rose's and Faith's stories, I thought about the themes they had chosen to address, looking in particular at the parts in the text that helped to develop those themes and the parts that did not. I thought about ways to help writers develop themes more clearly. My focus on theme is similar to Calkins's (1986) suggestion that teachers move away from a focus on *topic* as they help students revise. Calkins writes about helping two students who have relied too heavily on topic revisions:

> These children have not learned to experiment with the design and shape of their writing, but only to focus their topic. Focus has come to mean one thing only: selecting a smaller event. No one mentions thematic focus. Roberto does not know he could focus his piece around the reasons he loves watching sports. Carmel is unaware that she could eulogize her grandmother in a piece filled with wonderful memories of her. (p. 144)

Calkins's statement about thematic focus was most beneficial to students in my class. If Faith wrote about bullying, how could she best communicate that theme to her reader? When Rob wrote about popularity, he needed to make sure that this theme came through in his text. If the themes were weak or hidden, the social impact of the books would be lost. As an editor, developing the book's thematic power became my major focus.

Word-Processing Revisions

When students finished their rough drafts, I typed them, leaving spaces for students to add their revision. The word-processing revision strategy was very motivating for students because with each submission they could see their story looking more and more like a published document. The students loved getting their drafts back neatly typed. And rather than waiting for a teacher conference, they would go right to work, reading and responding to the comments on their draft. I offered suggestions, asked questions, and pushed students to add snapshots or metaphors and, generally, work the story as if it were a lump of clay to be molded and remolded (Kamler, 2001). Kamler calls on teachers to engage in "claywork" with student writers:

> This demands a more active engagement with the student on the page, not through teacherly margin notes or a running monologue at the front of the classroom, but by showing, by moving spatially, by taking the student text apart and putting it back together. The aim is to create greater agency for the writer and reposition her as a textworker, someone who can work actively and consciously...to shape the body of a text. (p. 178)

Rose's story was about a short girl who was teased about her height by another girl in her class. The girl teased her two times during the day. During their last class, music, the teacher announces, "We're going to be playing limbo today." Of course, the short girl wins handily. Cute idea, but more of a gag than a book.

Using a word-processing program, I typed Rose's story exactly as she had written it, leaving gaps and white space between scenes or time shifts. In each gap, I entered a question or suggestion and saved the draft on the computer hard drive. When I returned the typed draft to Rose the next day, I asked her to look through my comments and respond in the white spaces (see Figure 11a).

Rose went to work, reading through the draft, adding more text on each page. The new format made it easier for Rose to add new ideas. At the end of workshop, she would give her revised book back to me, and I would add her handwritten revisions to the typed draft, which was saved on the computer (see Figure 11b). This process continued daily as I added fewer suggestions to the draft each day, and Rose had fewer gaps to fill in. Rose ended up with five drafts; most students had at least three drafts, which was another departure

FIGURE 11a.   First Draft: Rose's Story

Story

~~One day on my~~ ~~I go~~ *went* to school. It was really early so I was one of the first ones at
school. (Leads, snapshots) *Two other people wear that* and *Kelly.*

Kelly was my frend but nether
always tesed me *while my class today*

I'm happy because today I'm going ice skating. But I'm even happier

because our class gets to go to music today.

We were going on a
Fild trip, *at the end of the day*

I am excited to go to music today because we get to do the limbo.
When I got to my class room ~~Bully~~ *nather* started calling me short. (Let's work to make this more exciting, more
descriptive.)

I went to go
say Ih to Kelly

from my past expectation that students would move from rough draft to final
draft after only one teacher conference.

During the project, we worked with the entire text, working over and over
again to revise. I worked in partnership with my student writers, as a good
editor would. One of my suggestions to Rose was to list a variety of insults made
to small people rather than repeating one over and over again in the story.

"Like what?" Rose asked.

"I don't know. Does anyone say 'half-pint' anymore?"

Rose started laughing and walked back to her desk. Within seconds, a
group of students crowded around her offering suggestions such as "shortie,"

FIGURE 11b. Second Draft: Rose's Story

> One Wednesday morning, I walked to school. I felt happy because we
> were going ice skating for a class field trip. But I was even happier because
> our class goes to music on Wednesdays. I was excited to go to music
> because we were going to play "Limbo."
>
> It was really early so I was one of the first ones to get to my classroom
> Two other kids were in my class, Heather and Kelly. Kelly was my friend,
> but Heather always teased me. I walked up to say hi to Kelly. hather
> wodent Let me in the door.
> hey Shirow whar are you
> going. I'm saing ih to Kelly
> The teacher came in. heather
> weat of to the teacher and said
> Bully started calling me short. (Let's work to make this more exciting! Can I
> more descriptive.)
> help
> you whih
> Soon we got
> The food
> on the bus
> theefood.

"shrimpo," and "small fry." Classmates got in on the act and helped Rose
revise her story, drawing on elements of kid culture to improve the quality of
her text (see Figure 11c).

Circle Check Out

At the end of our writing time, I no longer used Author's Chair to share
students' writing. Instead, we ended writer's workshop with Circle Check Out,
meeting in a circle on the rug with our writing and folders in front of us. If the
minilesson for that day had been on snapshots, each student found a snapshot

FIGURE 11c.   Final Draft: Rose's Story

Title: **Shorter then ever**

One Wednesday morning, I walked to school. I felt happy because we were going ice skating for a class field trip. But I was even happier because our class goes to music on Wednesdays. I was excited to go to music because we were going to play "Limbo."

It was really early so I was one of the first ones to get to my classroom Two other kids were in my class, Heather and Kelly. Kelly was my friend, but Heather always teased me. I walked up to say hi to Kelly. Heather blocked the doorway. "Hey shrimpo! Where are you going?" she asked me.

"I'm saying hi to Kelly,"

Just then the teacher came in. Heather walked up to the teacher and asked, "Can I help you with the food for the food drive?" Kelly and I went to our desks.

At 10:00, we got on the bus for the field trip. Heather sat in the seat behind Kelly and me. She kept teasing me about my height.

At the ice skating rink, we stood in line for skates. Heather came up to me, "What size skates are you getting? Size one?" Everybody laughed, except for Kelly and me. I felt like I wanted to go home.

to share. If students didn't have an example of a minilesson concept, they would read a selection of text that excited them.

Because there were 20 students, I told them to be prepared to share only a brief selection at their turn. I, too, would share a short selection of my writing. When I initiated Circle Check Out, I was thinking primarily of Lensmire's (1994) comments about how risky it is for some students to share their writing with classmates. I also thought about the survey responses (see chapter 2). But Circle Check Out had an unanticipated benefit in that students learned about great writing from one another. They heard the best parts of each student's story each day. After several Circle Check Out sessions, I began to notice small borrowings occurring. One day, when Danny was almost done with his book, he told me, "I'm changing my lead. I liked what Rob did at Circle Check Out yesterday." Circle Check Out ended up being a broad demonstration of strong writing. The students often responded to each writer with a short burst of spontaneous applause.

As more students shared and every voice was heard in some way, we were given more opportunities to learn about writing from the other writers in the class. However, the best thing about Circle Check Out—as opposed to Author's Chair—was that it wasn't a place for funny monologues and comedy routines. There was no pressure to be entertaining. Although parts of many students' picture books were humorous, Circle Check Out was a time to share our strongest writing and to demonstrate our experiments with the writing craft.

Concluding Thoughts

Writer's workshop developed a different look and feel after my revisions to its format. Students used history trail texts as writing resources. They also borrowed ideas from one another as they wrote. As a result of reading more about actual collaborations between authors and editors, I began to revise student writing more intensively. Working in partnership with the students as their editor, I emphasized the importance of revising several times before publication. I also held students more accountable for integrating minilesson concepts into their stories. By incorporating Circle Check Out, I provided additional opportunities for students to learn from classmates as they experimented with the fiction genre. These changes enhanced the quality of student writing, but just as important, these changes brought students together as collaborative members of a writer's collective.

CHAPTER 8

Complicating Classroom Life

A s students worked on their picture books, I began to notice that they occasionally talked about social issues while writing. The talk was enthusiastic—buoyant and boisterous. Issues of race and culture were raised during writer's workshop again and again. Sometimes I brought up these issues and sometimes the students did. Conversations were generated as a result of questions and misconceptions that arose during the writing of the picture books. Building the curriculum around issues of fairness worked to complicate life in the classroom. The stories written during writer's workshop also became more complex.

Are Chinese People White?

As I worked with Rob on his story one day, I noticed that he had taken up many elements of John's experiences with racism. Rob's main character was a Chinese boy who enjoys popularity because he owns a huge collection of Pokémon cards. The boy's popularity ends one day when his friends find out that he is Chinese. I asked Rob, "Don't you think the kids would know he was Chinese?"

"No. Chinese people look just the same as us. Look at John, he's white. His dad doesn't look different. He looks like everyone else. I can't even tell he's Chinese."

John came running over. "People say that Chinese people are 'yellow,' but that's not true. Chinese people don't have different skin color."

I said to John, "But Asian people do have specific features, don't you think? There are physical differences between different groups of people?"

Rob cut in, "No, there aren't."

John said, "Well, Chinese people do have differences, but it's not yellow skin."

John and Rob are good friends. When John bravely went public with his grievance about being called "Chinese Boy" at recess, he implicated not only the perpetrators (who were not in our class) but all the bystanders as well. Rob focused on John's story in his social narrative, perhaps, as a way to find his voice as a witness to racism.

When John went back to writing, I asked Rob, "Do you think that the characters in your book would know that the main character is Chinese by looking at him?"

Rob thought for a long while, "Do you think I could make him half Chinese and half white like John? It might be harder to tell."

I said, "Sure. And maybe when the characters find out, they would call him 'Chinese Boy' just like the kids at our school have done to John on the soccer field."

I remember not feeling totally comfortable with this conversation at the time, and I have experienced this sense of discomfort many times as part of work with critical literacy. Moments such as these don't have neat and tidy answers. These two 9-year-old boys were working together to try to understand race and racism as they worked on their stories. Writing social narratives required writers like Rob to make inquiries and to revise ideas.

Constructing Characters

Min frequently wrote about being Vietnamese as she wrote notebook entries in connection with history trail texts. One day, Min wrote in her notebook about her life in Vietnam before being adopted. She brought a picture of the orphanage and taped it into her notebook. When she finished reading it to us, there was silence. Then Drew spoke up, "I knew you were adopted, but I didn't know you lived in an orphanage."

Later that day when students were working on their books, I noticed Drew talking to some of his friends. He said, "I'm going to make the kid Vietnamese." He wrote this detail into the margins of his first page.

The stories of Min and John, who had experienced racism firsthand, influenced five other students to write about characters of a different ethnicity than they were. This surprised me because I had never seen student writers do this in the past. However, it provided us with opportunities to discuss our perceptions and misperceptions about culture and race. Many of the students I teach have led somewhat sheltered lives and have limited vocabulary when it comes to discussing social issues. Over the years, several students have revealed confusion about racial identity with comments such as "I have an African American friend in another class. Her name is Shin-young Choi." Because race is sometimes a taboo subject even for adults, the students are often relieved to be given even basic information about it. One day during writer's workshop, Devra asked, "Have you ever seen a woman wearing a red dot on her forehead? Because I saw someone like that at the mall."

Drew added, "Yeah, there's all kinds of people, and then you watch TV and there's like only one black person and all the rest of the people are white."

Although critical literacies do serve to "enhance everyday life in schools" (Comber, 2001, p. 1), critical literacy practices also enhance classroom life by *complicating* it. In my class, issues in books and issues in and outside of school became resources for student writers that led to an unusual complexity in their picture books.

Complicating Our Stories

Each student's story appeared to incorporate some combination of three different classroom events: notebook entries, class conversations, and ideas from the picture books themselves. The resulting combinations gave the books a complexity and richness that made them interesting reading material for me, for students in the class, and for students in other classes. The students had come a long way from their first pieces in the fall. When I had invited them to write about their passions, I received 20 pieces—all very straightforward and all less than one page long—about Pokémon, sports, and pets. These pieces did not include references to other texts or events in the way their picture books did. This intertextuality points to the importance of supplying student writers with a new set of textual references in writer's workshop.

Min incorporated three notebook entries in her book, "A Whole New Day"—entries about talks with her mom, a game called "Truths" that she played with kids in her neighborhood, and a kid at school making fun of her face (see Figure 12a). She also drew ideas from *Voices in the Park* (Browne, 1998) and our subsequent talk about gender segregation. Min's first draft had two girl main characters, but Min decided to change one of the characters to a boy. She told me, "I'm going to change the girl into a boy because then I'll have the skin color thing and the girl–boy thing."

Rob's book, "Hey, Popular Kid! It's Opposite Day," is about a boy who comes to a new school and becomes very popular because of his huge collection of rare Pokémon cards (see Figure 12b). When his new friends discover that he is biracial, they reject him. Only one other child, a short kid who no one especially likes, continues to be his friend. I surmised that Rob might have drawn from numerous events as he wrote his book:

FIGURE 12a.   Sample Picture Book Pages: Min

Mom was right. I felt much better the next day. The morning at school went great. I was having a wonderful day until recess. I was playing soccer. Third and fourth graders were playing together on the hot soccer field. I was inside the goal. I tried to make a goal, but I missed. A fourth grader named Zack ran up to me. In front of everyone he yelled, "You're ugly, and your face looks like a dead raccoon's face. And your skin is too brown." When he said that, I burst into tears. I dropped to the ground. I was shocked about what he had said to me.

That afternoon, I talked to my mom again. She said, "Try to work it out."

I said, "Okay."

FIGURE 12b. Sample Picture Book Pages: Rob

At recess, Brian walked up to Julie. "Do you want to play today?"

"I can't Chinese Boy," she answered and ran away.

Brian turned to Rachel. "Do you want to come over this afternoon, Rachel?"

"N.O. spells NO!" said Rachel.

"Do you want to play soccer, Tom?"

"Sure!"

They had a ball. Tom turned out to be a really good soccer player.

- Notebook entry about being teased on the soccer field
- Conversations about the Pokémon craze
- Conversations about popularity after reading *Creativity* and *Crow Boy*
- Conversation with John and me about the features of Chinese people

Concluding Thoughts

New conversations took place in the writer's workshop, about justice, difference, status, and power. A more complex workshop led to more complex stories as students wove together their personal lives and their social purposes. Kamler (2001) writes about the importance of relocating "individual meaning in wider social purposes" (pp. 7–8). This ability to relocate experience came about in my classroom as a result of my students and I talking about books and talking about our lives. Curricular conversations around published and student-generated texts supplied student writers with a new kind of writing resource and opened space for putting the stuff of our shared lives to work. Conversation, a rare commodity in schools today, brought a critical perspective to writer's workshop.

CHAPTER 9

Social Narratives: Bridging Personal Lives and Social Purposes

The social-narrative picture books were vastly different from the personal narratives that the students wrote at the beginning of the school year. Rather than sharing memories or observations of personal events, the students used fiction to analyze problems that occur when students enter the world called *school*. Within the school settings in their books, the students explored myriad issues such as status, authority, racism, gender stereotyping, bullying, anti-Semitism, friendship, and culture clash. These texts were sociological works, used to explore differences and power.

Characteristics of Social Narratives

In my work with Mitzi Lewison (2003), we described the emerging genre of social-narrative writing in the following way:

> Social-narrative writing does not reject the personal, but rather builds on it. Blending the personal and the social into fictional texts makes social narrative a hybrid genre, one that may bring power and purpose to Writer's Workshop as student writers come together to discover and share cultural themes and social issues. (p. 442)

In writing social narratives, student writers in this class

- shared cultural resources as they took on the identities, dilemmas, and obstacles of self and others,
- used fiction writing as a tool for constructing and analyzing shared social worlds,
- participated in making Writer's Workshop a writing collective in which writing is viewed as a form of social action, a vehicle for broadcasting messages to others. (p. 438)

Sharing Cultural Resources

Students in past years seemed to have two primary sources of textual reference—popular culture and personal events. They relied primarily on popular culture for writing material, copying stories that they knew from television, movies, and popular book series such as Goosebumps or Animorphs. When I placed restrictions on popular culture as a writing resource, students came up with other school writing topics with which they were familiar, producing texts about pets, vacations, and ball games. As we worked with critical texts, students had a new set of references for their writing. Although I anticipated that the writer's notebook entries would be used as their primary reference material, the students used a combination of ideas from the social-issue texts, their notebook entries, and classroom conversations for composing their books. This blending of references made students' picture books more complex and creative than fiction I have worked with in the past.

Perhaps the most significant resource for students was talk. Without an emphasis on classroom conversation, the sociological aspect of students' writing would have been lost. Drew would never have changed his main character from a white child to a Vietnamese child if he had not heard Min speaking about the orphanage in which she lived in Vietnam. Devra would never have included an overweight student in her book if Joshua had never told us all, "They call me fat." Alex probably would never have written about boys and girls being friends if we had not discussed our own experiences with being teased about this. And John would never have had the opportunity to tell us how he felt when boys yelled "Chinese Boy" at him nearly every day on the soccer field.

Writing to Construct and Analyze Shared Social Worlds

The playground politics of recess appeared in 18 of the 20 books (which teachers will not find surprising). Recess is somewhat of a microcosm of the larger social world and a good place to look at the ways in which people position themselves against one another. The students knew that bullying, teasing, excluding, and even racism occurred at recess on a daily basis. Writing about recess gave them opportunities to analyze playground politics.

Against the backdrop of recess, there were many social and political issues that were developed through the students' stories. Surprisingly, the books were not gender specific in terms of theme, as writing so often is in writer's workshop. Boys had boy main characters and girls had girl main characters. But all the students had stories of boys and girls experiencing the same kinds of issues and doing the same kinds of things—trying to cope with competition and pressure during soccer games, walking around at recess with nothing to do, making friends, and breaking down in tears.

Students' writing portrayed recess as a lawless place, where aggression broke out randomly and rampantly. Students pointed to the ongoing problems at recess with "this went on for months" and "I told him not to do it, but he didn't stop. I asked him again and again and again" (Heffernan & Lewison, 2003, p. 439). Student writers, particularly critical of adults at school, pointed out the failure of those in authority to deal with injustice:

> I tried to make a goal, but I missed. A fourth grader named Zack ran up to me. In front of everyone he yelled, "You're ugly and your face looks like a dead raccoon's face. And your skin is too brown." When he said that, I burst into tears. I dropped to the ground. I was shocked about what he had said to me. (Min)

> When they were allowed to go back to class, Lance started crying. He was still crying when he got to his classroom. He told his teacher how they had won and about the way Gary had teased him. The teacher said he could do nothing about it. (John)

> Whenever the teachers at school weren't looking, bullies always teased him at Hoover School. (Alex)

Because students were able to talk and write about their common experiences with teasing, bullying, and other issues, they gained some distance from these experiences by questioning the institutions of school and recess rather than regarding themselves as deficient in some way.

Writer's Collective: We're Writing to Change the World

A shared sense of purpose dramatically changed the atmosphere of writer's workshop. At the beginning of the year, survey results showed that students overwhelmingly believed that the purpose of writing in school is to make better writers. In the past, my goals for writer's workshop had been to give students opportunities to choose their topics and to mine their own lives for interesting tales to share and to go through the process of taking a story from idea to final draft. My former approach to writer's workshop communicated to students that they were there to express themselves but without any guidelines or support for expressing their feelings about social issues—those events in our lives that trouble or confuse us and that we care about strongly. By the end of the school year, however, when the students were asked to write about their writing process and purpose, they had this to say:

> Hi, I'm a writer. I write about differences…I think people should read my book because when they read it they will learn not to make fun of other people. I have been made fun of. Because I'm different. People should treat others the way they want to be treated.
>
> I have a connection with *Creativity*. The boy in *Creativity* is different like I am. (Min, in "A Whole New Day")

> Hi my name is Gregory and I have been teased nearly all my life because I'm small. But a book named *Crow Boy* inspired me to treat others the way we want to be treated. In the book, Crow Boy was teased because he's small, but in the end, they all see that they have been very mean to Crow Boy. Being small can be fun, but it doesn't matter about the size you are. (Gregory, in "Connor and Dylan")

> I am a writer. I am writing about teasing. Teasing is a bad thing to do. Teasing is a problem in our school. *Crow Boy* inspired me to write about teasing.
>
> *Crow Boy* is about a boy who was teased because he was small. Teasing someone because they're small makes no sense. Because even if they're small doesn't automatically make them bad. I once was teased because my hair was tangley. It doesn't feel good. I hope you read and like my book. (Faith, in "Carrot Head")

> I wrote a book called Being Lonely. *Ramona's World* inspired me to write about being lonely. When Ms. Heffernan read it, it made me think. And in some of it, it made me wonder what would happen if boys and girls got to be friends. My book is about a boy named Sam who is being teased and hurt. And a girl comes in and tries to play with him. They become best friends. I think boys and girls should be friends. I hope you read my book. (Alex, in "Being Lonely")

> Everyone is different in some way. Some are more different than others are. I wrote this book about differences and teasing because people like me are teased because of their skin color. I also wrote it to tell you that you can't judge a person by the way they look. I was inspired to write this book because in a

book, *Crow Boy*, one boy was left alone, always the tag-along. *Crow Boy* is related to my book because it's almost the same thing, only from my life. (John, in "New Friends")

I am a writer. I think we should tell people it is not good to tease. I learned from John Steptoe and *Creativity*. I think that if we could care for each other it would make the world better. Just think what it would be like if we cared about each other. (Rob, in "Hey, Popular Kid—It's Opposite Day")

Writer's workshop became a collective as a result of a curriculum based on conversation, the implementation of more inclusive workshop structures, and the recognition of a shared sense of purpose as students collectively engaged in meaningful work.

Teacher as Activist in the Writer's Workshop

Lensmire (1994) calls for "an increased role for teachers as curriculum-makers in writing classrooms" (p. 7). The increased role I took on as a writing teacher was one of an activist who introduced the students early in the school year to the notion that writing could be used as a way of interacting with readers to bring about social changes. I read books to the students about social issues and pointed out that authors used books to communicate important ideas. I listened for issues of inequity in conversations and highlighted these as events that concern all of us. I wrote my own book about the pressure I felt to coerce my son to conform to gender stereotypes. I shared excerpts from this book with students during Circle Check Out, telling them how writing the book had convinced me that I had to work harder to identify and reject societal pressures to conform. I responded to students' talk or writing that represented bias or prejudice. I made changes in the structure of writer's workshop so that the classroom would be a fairer place for student writers.

The students joined me in this role, pointing out issues in school of which I had no knowledge. Through their writing, the students took on issues that were upsetting or confusing to them. They eventually read their books to other classes, attempting to spread the word. The books were also posted on the school website. This writing project helped the students to reconsider some of their own actions. I will never forget the day that Drew, in the midst of an argument about table space, shouted to all of us, "Hey, if we act like this, we're like the bad characters in our books." The picture books became a form of social action for us, bringing students together to work for social changes.

Concluding Thoughts

In past classrooms, my students wrote outrageous and goofy fantasy stories, often about characters from television or movies. At first, I worked to teach students how to be better fiction writers. Eventually, I turned to personal narratives as a way to get students to explore issues from their own lives. These endeavors helped to improve overall writing quality, and writer's workshop became consistently popular among my students. A shift to critical literacy in writer's workshop, however, brought purpose and passion to student writing by providing students with the resources for connecting their personal and social worlds.

CHAPTER 10

Answering Questions About Critical Writer's Workshop

Four more classes of third graders have written social narratives in my class since the kids in this book left my classroom. Over the years, people have asked me two questions about working with critical literacy practices: (1) What do parents think about all this? and (2) You don't teach black children, do you?

To answer the first question, when I started working with social issue texts, I feared that parents might disapprove, but over the years, I've received only positive feedback. Parents have been especially impressed with their children's writing. One father came to school one day and asked me, "Did she really write that story?" When I told him about the process that went into the project, he replied, "I'm just so used to her writing stuff like 'I went to the fair. The fair was fun.' I couldn't believe she could write something like that. It's really good." Parents wrote positive comments in their portfolio responses as well: "I'm glad to see the emphasis put on writing this year" and "He worked so hard on his picture book. Way to go!" and "It's great to see content entering the curriculum."

After completing the picture books described in the previous chapters, students went on to work on a second picture book. As a resource for this writing, I read books about rights and social action to the students, hoping to make this second selection of books extend to the world outside of school. In response to these read-alouds, several children wrote historical fiction about slavery. The students knew, without help from me, which themes they wanted to explore. At first, this independence frustrated me. After all, I had a system and wanted to stick to it. Eventually, I came to appreciate the way in which the students had become writers with stories they wanted to write and share.

At the end of the school year described in the previous chapters, I received a letter from a parent about her son's writing.

Lee,

I wanted to let you know how much the writing about social issues has impacted Rob. He has talked non-stop about writing his picture books. He has taken more interest in writing these books than I have ever seen him do. He told us that studying about slavery has changed his life. We were floored.

    I appreciate all of your hard work and the love of reading and writing that you have shared with Rob. He has truly become an inspired writer.

Although in the future I may have some parents who ask questions or share concerns, and I'm hopeful that they will, I do not believe that parents will complain about their children creating wonderful stories. Parents want their children to grow as writers and readers. Adding a sociological perspective to writer's workshop gives students the opportunity to write powerfully and with a sense of purpose. It helps students generate new meaning and understanding through their writing. I think parents are thrilled when they see their kids learning to do something challenging and new.

The second question confused me for a long time: You don't teach black children, do you? Over and over again, I have heard variations of this question. It's troubling to think that people believe that exploration of race or other social issues is not relevant to the lives of middle class white children. Several teachers have asked how these conversations can be handled in classrooms with only a few children of color because they worry that these children might feel embarrassed or singled out when social issues are read about and discussed. In my experience thus far, this has not been a problem, but making curricular choices based on class-generated themes does help to determine the level of student interest in social issues. Each class of students has generated their own themes in their conversations and social narratives, taking up such topics as ageism, consumerism, and gender segregation. The enthusiasm that students have displayed for this work has led me to believe that all students want and need opportunities to explore issues of difference and justice.

The world does not offer easy answers or simple stories. "Disrupting the commonplace" in writer's workshop allows students to complicate their stories and connect with their readers.

References

Atwell, N. (1987). *In the middle: Writing, reading, and learning with adolescents.* Portsmouth, NH: Boynton/Cook.

Calkins, L. (1986). *The art of teaching writing.* Portsmouth, NH: Heinemann.

Coles, G. (1998). *Reading lessons: The debate over literacy.* New York: Farrar Straus Giroux.

Comber, B. (2001). Negotiating critical literacies. *School Talk, 6*(3), 1–2.

Comber, B., & Cormack, P. (1995). *Analyzing early literacy teaching practices.* Adelaide, SA, Australia: Department for Education and Children's Services.

Freire, P. (1998). *Teachers as cultural workers: Letters to those who dare teach.* New York: Westview Press.

Graves, D. (1983). *Writing: Teachers and children at work.* Portsmouth, NH: Heinemann.

Harste, J.C., & Leland, C. (2000). Critical literacy: Enlarging the space of the possible. *Primary Voices K–6, 9*(2), 3–7.

Harste, J.C., Short, K.G., & Burke, C.L. (1988). *Creating classrooms for authors: The reading-writing connection.* Portsmouth, NH: Heinemann.

Harste, J.C., & Vasquez, V. (1998). The work we do: Journal as audit trail. *Language Arts, 75*(4), 266–276.

Heffernan, L., & Lewison, M. (2000). Making real-world issues our business: Critical literacy in a third grade classroom. *Primary Voices K–6, 9*(2), 15–21.

Heffernan, L., & Lewison, M. (2003). Social narrative writing: (Re)constructing kid culture in the writer's workshop. *Language Arts, 80*(6), 435–443.

Kamler, B. (1993). Constructing gender in the process writing classroom. *Language Arts, 70,* 95–103.

Kamler, B. (2001). *Relocating the personal: A critical writing pedagogy.* Albany: State University of New York Press.

Kohl, H.R. (1995). *Should we burn Babar? Essays on children's literature and the power of stories.* New York: The New Press.

Lane, B. (1993). *After the end: Teaching and learning creative revision.* Portsmouth, NH: Heinemann.

Lankshear, C., & McLaren, P. (Eds.). (1993). *Critical literacy: Politics, praxis and the postmodern.* Albany: State University of New York Press.

Leland, C.H., Harste J.C., Oceipka, A., Lewison, M., & Vasquez, V. (1999). Exploring critical literacy: You can hear a pin drop. *Language Arts, 77*(1), 70–77.

Lensmire, T.J. (1994). *When children write: Critical re-visions of the writing workshop.* New York: Teachers College Press.

Lewison, M., Seely-Flint, A., & Van Sluys, K. (2002). Taking on critical literacy: The journey of newcomers and novices. *Language Arts, 79*(5), 382–392.

Luke, A., & Freebody, P. (1997). Shaping the social practices of reading. In S. Muspratt & A. Luke (Eds.), *Constructing critical literacies: Teaching and learning textual practice* (pp. 185–225). Cresskill, NJ: Hampton Press.

Shannon, P. (1995). *Text, lies & videotape: Stories about life, literacy, and learning.* Portsmouth, NH: Heinemann.

Short, K.G., Harste, J.C., & Burke, C.L. (1996). *Creating classrooms for authors and inquirers* (2nd ed.). Portsmouth, NH: Heinemann.

Soo Hoo, S., & Brown, B. (1994). Developing voice in the democratic classroom. In S. Steffey & W.J. Hood (Eds.), *If this is social studies, why isn't it boring?* York, ME: Stenhouse.

Tatum, B.D. (1997). *"Why are all the black kids sitting together in the cafeteria?"* New York: Basic Books.

Wooldridge, S.G. (1996). *Poem crazy: Freeing your life with words.* New York: Three Rivers Press.

CHILDREN'S BOOK REFERENCES

Bloomington Human Rights Commission Essay Contest. [Brochure]. (1999). Bloomington, IN: City of Bloomington.

Blumberg, R. (1996). *Bloomers.* Ill. M. Morgan. New York: Simon & Schuster.

Browne, A. (1998). *Voices in the park.* New York: Dorling Kindersley.

Bulla, C.R. (1989). *A lion to guard us.* Ill. M. Chessare. New York: HarperTrophy.

Bunting, E. (1996). *Going home.* Ill. D. Diaz. New York: HarperCollins.

Bunting, E. (with D'Andrader, D., Ed.). (1998). *Your move.* Ill. T. Rasome. New York: Harcourt Brace.

Burch, R. (with Brodies, D., Ed.). (1990). *Ida Early comes over the mountain.* New York: Puffin.

Cairo, S., Cairo, J., & Cairo, T. (1985). *Our brother has Down's Syndrome: An introduction for children.* Chicago: Firefly.

Cleary, B. (1999). *Ramona's world.* Ill. A. Tiegreen. New York: Morrow.

Coerr, E. (1979). *Sadako and the thousand paper cranes.* Ill. R. Himler. New York: Yearling.

Fletcher, R. (1998). *Flying solo.* Boston: Houghton Mifflin.

Giblin, J.C. (1986). *Milk: The fight for purity.* New York: HarperCollins.

Hansen, J. (1998). *Women of hope.* New York: Scholastic.

Hesse, K. (1996). *The music of dolphins.* New York: Scholastic.

Hesse, K. (1998). *Just Juice.* Ill. R.A. Parker. New York: Scholastic.

High rents in Bloomington. (1999, January). *The Herald-Times*, n.p.

Kaplan, W., & Tanaka, S. (1998). *One more border: The true story of one family's wartime escape from war-torn Europe.* Ill. S. Taylor. New York: Douglas & McIntyre.

Kosovo's sorrow. (1999, April 16). *Time for Kids*, *4*(23), p. 2.

Krull, K. (1996). *Wilma unlimited: How Wilma Rudolph became the world's fastest woman.* New York: Harcourt Brace.

Lauber, P. (1990). *Lost star: The story of Amelia Earhart*. New York: Scholastic.

Lears, L. (1998). *Ian's walk: A story about autism*. Ill. K. Ritz. Chicago: Albert Whitman.

Lester, J. (1998). *From slave ship to freedom road*. Ill. R. Brown. New York: Puffin.

Lindbergh, R. (1999). *Nobody owns the sky*. New York: Econo-Clad.

MacLachlan, P. (1987). *Sarah, plain and tall*. New York: HarperTrophy.

MacLachlan, P. (1997). *Skylark*. New York: HarperTrophy.

McCully, E.A. (1996). *The bobbin girl*. New York: Dial.

McGuffee, M. (1997). *The day the earth was silent*. Ill. E. Sullivan. Bloomington, IN: Inquiring Voices Press.

Mochizuki, K. (1997). *Passage to freedom: The Sugihara story*. New York: Lee & Low.

Namioka, L. (1994). *Yang the Youngest and his terrible ear*. New York: Yearling.

Shange, N. (1997). *Whitewash*. Ill. M. Sporn. New York: Walker & Company.

Steptoe, J. (1997). *Creativity*. Ill. E. Lewis. Boston: Houghton Mifflin.

Surat, M.S. (1989). *Angel child, dragon child*. Ill. V.D. Mai. New York: Scholastic.

Van Allsburg, C. (1988). *Two bad ants*. Boston: Houghton Mifflin.

Wright, C.C. (1994). *Journey to freedom*. Ill. G. Griffith. New York: Holiday House.

Yashima, T. (1976). *Crow Boy*. New York: Puffin.

Index

Note: Page numbers followed by *f* indicate figures and by *t* indicate tables.